PASSOVER HAGGADAH

by

RABBI NATHAN GOLDBERG

LARGE TYPE
NUMBERED LINES
TRANSLATION • TRANSLITERATION

KTAV PUBLISHING HOUSE INC.

copyright © 2006
ISBN 978-0-88125-913-1
KTAV PUBLISHING HOUSE
527 Empire Blvd.
Brooklyn, NY 11225

Website: www.ktav.com
Email: orders@ktav.com
Ph: (718)972-5449 / Fax: (718)972-6307

Printing year: 2019

TABLE OF CONTENTS

THE STORY OF PASSOVER

The Exodus

How does this night differ from all other nights? On all other nights we eat bread and matzah; why on this night do we eat only matzah?

We were slaves to Pharaoh in Egypt; and Moses was sent to free our people from bondage...

The question is the same every year, and so is the answer. For both are part of a ceremony that has remained unchanged for centuries upon centuries. This ceremony is called the *Seder,* and it marks the beginning of Passover.

What is Passover?

Passover, or Pesach, is many things. It is a festival of freedom, when we recall how the Almighty released our ancestors from slavery in Egypt and helped a free people come into existence.

Passover is an agricultural festival, reminding us of the land of Israel in ancient times. Our ancestors were farmers, and Passover marked the beginning of the grain harvest.

Passover is also a pilgrimage festival. Three times a year, the Israelites went in joyous procession to Jerusalem, to celebrate the festivals of Passover, Shavuot, and Sukkot.

Passover is all of these things, but it is especially a holiday for children. Our ancestors were instructed: "You shall tell it to your child." The Seder service, the reading of the Haggadah, the Four Questions, the stealing of the afikomen-all these are meant for boys and girls, to teach them the importance of this great holiday in the history of the Jewish people.

Turn Back the Clock

To learn the story of Pesach we must wend our way across the sands of time to a distant age and a strange land. There, in ancient Egypt, lived Joseph, the favorite and gifted son of Jacob. Joseph had been sold by his brothers to Midianite merchants, who in turn had brought him to Egypt.

One day Joseph was thrown into prison on false charges. Soon afterwards, Pharaoh, the ruler of Egypt, had a strange dream in which seven lean cows devoured seven fat ones. Not a single wise man or wizard in all the land could tell the meaning of the dream. Then Joseph, who had interpreted dreams for the royal cupbearer and the royal baker, was called before the Pharaoh.

"I have dreamed a dream and none can interpret it," said the Pharaoh.

Joseph answered, "God is the interpreter of dreams. Perhaps through me He shall grant the Pharaoh peace of mind."

Joseph listened and then told the Pharaoh that his dream meant that seven years of famine would follow seven years of plenty in the land of Egypt.

The Pharaoh rewarded Joseph by making him governor over all the land.

The new governor built huge granaries to be filled during the years of plenty. When the years of famine came, the full granaries saved Egypt from starvation.

Hyksos in Egypt

A time of famine came to Canaan, and the thoughts of the patriarch Jacob turned longingly to the fertile land of the Nile, where food was plentiful, even as other countries experienced famine. At Joseph's invitation, Jacob brought his family and flocks to Egypt.

The Pharaoh assigned the territory of Goshen to the Israelites. It was good grazing land, and for many years the Israelites lived there in peace.

Some historians believe that these events occurred around 1700 B.C.E., during the time when the Hyksos, a warlike tribe from Syria, swept into Egypt. The Hyksos ruled Egypt for about 120 years. Joseph was probably a high-ranking official under one of these powerful foreign rulers.

Slaves of the Pharaoh

Eventually the Hyksos were defeated, and Egyptian kings once more ruled over the land. The new Pharaohs, as the Bible tells us, "did not know Joseph." No longer were the Israelites respected as the privileged descendants of a noble ancestor. The Pharaohs had great need for slaves to build new cities and magnificent palaces so they were enslaved. Some historians believe that this took place during the reign of Rameses II (ca. 1290-1224 B.C.E.). Egypt was a growing empire at this time, and Rameses feared an uprising among the slaves and took cruel precautions to prevent it.

He issued a decree that all male children born to the Israelites must be killed. In this merciless way, Rameses hoped to keep the Israelites from growing in numbers.

Baby Moses

Soon after this decree was issued, a male child was born to Jochebed, an Israelite woman, and her husband, Amram, of the tribe of Levi. To save the infant, they put him in a basket and set him afloat among the bulrushes of the Nile.

The baby was found by an Egyptian princess while she and her handmaidens were bathing in the river.

The princess called the baby Moses, which means, "drawn out of the water."

As a boy, Moses was given all the advantages enjoyed by members of Egypt's Royal family.

One day Moses, now a prince, was outraged to see an Egyptian overseer beating an Israelite slave. Moses killed the Egyptian overseer and fled to the land of Midian in the Sinai desert. There he became a shepherd, living with the Kenite priest named Jethro. Moses married Jethro's daughter Zipporah, who bore him two sons.

The Burning Bush

In the rugged mountains of Sinai, Moses had an inspiring experience. Through a vision of a burning bush that was not consumed, God told him to go down to Egypt, confront Pharaoh, and lead the slaves to freedom. At first Moses refused, but eventually he accepted the responsibility. From that time forward, Moses was a man dedicated to the great task of leading his people to freedom.

Many obstacles were placed in his path by the Pharaoh. Again and again Moses, accompanied by his brother Aaron, stood before Pharaoh and pleaded for the Israelites. Pharaoh, full of power turned a deaf ear to his pleas.

Ten Plagues

Egypt had to be stricken by ten disastrous plagues before Pharaoh, finally consented to release the Israelites and allow them to leave the land. A multitude of about 600,000 men, in addition to women and children left Egypt on that memorable night of the Exodus. There was barely time to prepare the food they would need.

The Israelites left so hurriedly that they had no time to bake their bread. They spread the raw unleavened dough on pieces of wood and tied them to their shoulders.

The hot desert sun baked the dough into matzot. This was the origin of the law of eating unleavened bread (matzot) on Passover, the festival that commemorates the victory won for freedom so many centuries ago.

The Exodus: A March to Freedom

So the great march out of Egypt began with families gathered together, each with its own tribe, twelve tribes in all. However, Pharaoh suddenly changed his mind and sent charioteers to bring the slaves back.

The march was halted suddenly by an obstacle that seemed to be insurmountable. Silent and disheartened the Israelites stood, the light of hope slowly fading from their eyes as they gazed at the vast expanse of water before them. They had come to the end of dry land, to the shores of the Sea of Reeds (Yam Suf), the Suez arm of the Red Sea.

Those who looked back in the direction of their former homes were greeted by a sight that chilled their already sinking hearts. Bearing down upon them was a column of Egyptian soldiers. With the sea before them and the army of Pharaoh closing in from behind, the Israelites were trapped.

Then, miraculously, a strong east wind rose. It drove back the waters of the sea, making a path of dry land. With joyful hearts, the throng followed Moses to the opposite shore. In fierce pursuit, Pharaoh's soldiers also took the dry path through the Sea of Reeds, but the wind turned and the tide rolled in. Back rushed the waters, engulfing the chariots and drowning the soldiers.

Free at Last

The Bible tells us of how the Israelites rejoiced when they found themselves safely across the sea. Moses composed a poem of praise to God. The women danced joyously to the music of their timbrels and sang a song composed by Miriam, Moses' sister. Ahead of them lay untold dangers, but on this great day there was but one song in the hearts of the Israelites, a song of gratitude for their newly won freedom.

The Israelites wandered for 40 years until they reached Canaan, the Promised Land beyond the river Jordan. In Canaan they began a new life. They built homes and planted vineyards, and celebrated their harvest festivals. Since those days, we begin the celebration of Pesach on the eve of the 15th day of Nisan. During the week of the festival (observed for seven days by Reform Jews and Israelis, for eight by others) we eat unleavened bread to remind us of the bread our ancestors baked in haste when they left the land of Pharaoh.

בְּדִיקַת חָמֵץ
SEARCHING FOR LEAVEN

On the evening following the thirteenth of Nisan (if the first day
of Passover is on Sunday, on the evening following the twelfth of
Nisan), after the evening service, the head of the household makes
the final preparation for Passover by searching for leaven throughout
the house. It is customary to place ten pieces of bread in various
places, so that when the search is made, leaven is found. Otherwise,
the benediction recited before the ceremony would be in vain.

Before the ceremony of searching for leaven begins, a candle
is lighted and the following prayer is recited:

1 **Barukh** ata Adonai Eloheynu melekh
haolam, asher kidshanu b'mitsvotav
v'tsivanu al biur khamets.

1 **בָּרוּךְ** אַתָּה יְיָ אֱלֹהֵינוּ מֶלֶךְ הָעוֹלָם, אֲשֶׁר
2 קִדְּשָׁנוּ בְּמִצְוֹתָיו, וְצִוָּנוּ עַל בְּעוּר חָמֵץ.

The search for leaven is conducted. After the leaven has been
gathered and wrapped securely, the following is said:

3 **Kol khamira** vakhamia d'ika vir'shuti dla
khamite udla viarte udla y'dana le libatel
v'lehevey hefker k'afra d'ara.

3 **כָּל חֲמִירָא** וַחֲמִיעָא דְּאִכָּא בִרְשׁוּתִי דְּלָא
4 חֲמִתֵּהּ וּדְלָא בְעַרְתֵּהּ וּדְלָא יְדַעְנָא לֵהּ לִבָּטֵל
5 וְלֶהֱוֵי הֶפְקֵר כְּעַפְרָא דְאַרְעָא.

On the fourteenth of Nisan (if the first day of Passover is on
Sunday, on the thirteenth of Nisan), about ten o'clock in the
morning, all the leaven that has remained in the house, together
with all collected during the search the previous night, is
burned. At the burning of the leaven the following is recited:

Kol khamira vakhamia d'ika vir'shuti
dakhazite udla khazite, dakhamite udla
khamite, d'viarte udla viarte, libatel
v'lehevey hefker k'afra d'ara.

6 **כָּל חֲמִירָא** וַחֲמִיעָא דְּאִכָּא בִרְשׁוּתִי דַּחֲזִתֵּהּ
7 וּדְלָא חֲזִתֵּהּ, דַּחֲמִתֵּהּ וּדְלָא חֲמִתֵּהּ, דְּבַעַרְתֵּהּ
8 וּדְלָא בְעַרְתֵּהּ, לִבָּטֵל וְלֶהֱוֵי הֶפְקֵר כְּעַפְרָא
9 דְאַרְעָא.

SEARCHING FOR LEAVEN

On the evening following the thirteenth of Nisan (if the first day
of Passover is on Sunday, on the evening following the twelfth of
Nisan), after the evening service, the head of the household makes
the final preparation for Passover by searching for leaven throughout
the house. It is customary to place ten pieces of bread in various
places, so that when the search is made, leaven is found. Otherwise,
the benediction recited before the ceremony would be in vain.

Before the ceremony of searching for leaven begins, a
candle is lighted and the following prayer is recited:

1 **Praised are You**, Eternal our God, Ruler of the universe, Who
made us holy with His commandments and commanded us
to remove the leaven.

The search for leaven is conducted. After the leaven has been
gathered and wrapped securely, the following is said:

3 **Any leaven** that may still be in the house, which I have not
seen or have not removed, shall be as if it does not exist, and
as the dust of the earth.

On the fourteenth of Nisan (if the first day of Passover is on
Sunday, on the thirteenth of Nisan), about ten o'clock in the
morning, all the leaven that has remained in the house, together
with all collected during the search the previous night, is
burned. At the burning of the leaven the following is recited:

6 **Any leaven** that may still be in the house, which I have or
have not seen, which I have or have not removed, shall be
as if it does not exist, and as the dust of the earth.

עֵרוּב תַּבְשִׁילִין
MIXING OF FOODS

When Passover falls on a Friday, in order that it may be permissible to
cook on that day for Saturday (one is permitted to cook on a holiday
for that day alone), the head of the household must perform the
ritual of "Eruv Tavshilin" before the festival. This consists of taking
some matzah and some other food, such as fish or meat, putting
them on a plate, raising it, and then reciting the following prayers:

1	**Barukh** ata Adonai, Eloheynu melekh haolam, asher kidshanu b'mitsotav, v'tsivanu al mitsvat eruv.	1 **בָּרוּךְ** אַתָּה יְיָ אֱלֹהֵינוּ מֶלֶךְ הָעוֹלָם, אֲשֶׁר 2 קִדְּשָׁנוּ בְּמִצְוֹתָיו, וְצִוָּנוּ עַל מִצְוַת עֵרוּב.
3	**Bahadeyn** eruva y'hey sharey lana laafuyey ulvashuley ulatmuney uladlukey shraga ultakana ulmebad kol tsarkhana, miyoma tava l'Shabatah lanu ul'khol Yisrael hadarim bair hazot.	3 **בַּהֲדֵין** עֵרוּבָא יְהֵא שָׁרֵא לָנָא לַאֲפוּיֵי וּלְבַשׁוּלֵי 4 וּלְאַטְמוּנֵי וּלְאַדְלוּקֵי שְׁרָגָא וּלְתַקָּנָא וּלְמֶעֱבַד 5 כָּל צָרְכָנָא, מִיּוֹמָא טָבָא לְשַׁבַּתָּא לָנוּ וּלְכָל 6 יִשְׂרָאֵל הַדָּרִים בָּעִיר הַזֹּאת.

דִּינֵי הַסֵּדֶר בְּלֵיל פֶּסַח
THE PREPARATION OF THE TABLE

Three plates are placed on the table; in one put three matzot; in
another, a shank bone, an egg, either roasted or cooked, some
horseradish ("bitter herbs"), celery or parsley, and a compound
formed of nuts, fruits, and wine (haroset); in a third, salt water.

Egg	Shank Bone	זְרוֹעַ	בֵּיצָה
	Bitter Herbs		מָרוֹר
Parsley	Haroset	חֲרוֹסֶת	כַּרְפַּס

4

MIXING OF FOODS

When Passover falls on a Friday, in order that it may be permissible to cook on that day for Saturday (one is permitted to cook on a holiday for that day alone), the head of the household must perform the ritual of "Eruv Tavshilin" before the festival. This consists of taking some matzah and some other food, such as fish or meat, putting them on a plate, raising it, and then reciting the following prayers:

1 **Praised are You**, Eternal our God, Ruler of the universe, Who made us holy with His commandments and commanded us concerning the *Eruv.*

3 **With this** *Eruv* it shall be permissible for us to bake, cook, and keep the food warm, to light the candles, and to prepare all necessary things on the festival for the Sabbath. This shall be permitted to us and to all Jews who live in this city.

THE PREPARATION OF THE TABLE

Three plates are placed on the table; in one put three matzot; in another, a shank bone, an egg, either roasted or cooked, some horseradish ("bitter herbs"), celery or parsley, and a compound formed of nuts, fruits, and wine (haroset); in a third, salt water.

Egg	Shank Bone		בֵּיצָה	זְרוֹעַ
	Bitter Herbs			מָרוֹר
Parsley	Haroset		כַּרְפַּס	חֲרוֹסֶת

5

סימן לסדר של פסח
ORDER OF THE PASSOVER SEDER

8. מָרוֹר **. Maror**

Eat the bitter herb.

1. קַדֵּשׁ **. Kadesh**

Recite the Kiddush.

9. כּוֹרֵךְ **. Korech**

Eat the bitter herb
and matzah together.

2. וּרְחַץ **. Urchatz**

Wash the hands.

10. שֻׁלְחָן עוֹרֵךְ **. Shulchan Orech**

Serve the Festival meal.

3. כַּרְפַּס **. Karpas**

Eat a green vegetable.

11. צָפוּן **. Tzafun**

Eat the Afikoman.

4. יַחַץ **. Yachatz**

Break the middle matzah and
hide a half for the Afikoman.

12. בָּרֵךְ **. Barech**

Say the grace after meal

5. מַגִּיד **. Magid**

Recite the Passover story.

13. הַלֵּל **. Hallel**

Recite the Hallel.

6. רָחְצָה **. Rachtza**

Wash the hands before the meal.

14. נִרְצָה **. Nirtza**

Conclude the Seder.

7. מוֹצִיא מַצָּה **. Motzi Matzah**

Say Hamotzi and the special
blessing for the matzah.

EGG

SHANK BONE

BITTER HERBS

PARSLEY

HAROSET

SEDER PLATE

קַדֵּשׁ KADESH

RECITATION OF THE KIDDUSH

The first cup of wine is poured.

THE FIRST CUP

On Friday night begin with the following paragraph:

Silently: Vay'hi erev vay'hi voker

בלחש: וַיְהִי עֶרֶב וַיְהִי בֹקֶר

1 **Yom hashishi**, vay'khulu hashamayim v'haarets v'khol tsvaam. Vay'khal Elohim bayom hash'vii, m'lakhto asher asa, vayishbot bayom hash'vii, mikol m'lakhto asher asa. Vay'varekh Elohim et yom hash'vii, vay'kadesh oto, ki vo shavat mikol m'lakhto, asher bara Elohim laasot.

1 **יוֹם הַשִּׁשִּׁי**, וַיְכֻלּוּ הַשָּׁמַיִם וְהָאָרֶץ וְכָל־צְבָאָם:

2 וַיְכַל אֱלֹהִים בַּיּוֹם הַשְּׁבִיעִי, מְלַאכְתּוֹ אֲשֶׁר

3 עָשָׂה, וַיִּשְׁבֹּת בַּיּוֹם הַשְּׁבִיעִי, מִכָּל־מְלַאכְתּוֹ

4 אֲשֶׁר עָשָׂה: וַיְבָרֶךְ אֱלֹהִים אֶת־יוֹם הַשְּׁבִיעִי,

5 וַיְקַדֵּשׁ אֹתוֹ, כִּי בוֹ שָׁבַת מִכָּל־מְלַאכְתּוֹ, אֲשֶׁר־

6 בָּרָא אֱלֹהִים לַעֲשׂוֹת:

Other nights of the week, begin here:

Savri maranan v'rabanan v'rabotai.

7 סַבְרִי מָרָנָן וְרַבָּנָן וְרַבּוֹתַי:

8 **Barukh ata Adonai**, Eloheynu Melekh Haolam, borey pri hagafen.

8 **בָּרוּךְ** אַתָּה יְיָ, אֱלֹהֵינוּ מֶלֶךְ הָעוֹלָם, בּוֹרֵא פְּרִי

9 הַגָּפֶן:

On Shabbat, add the words in parentheses:

Barukh ata Adonai, Eloheynu Melekh Haolam, Haolam, asher bakhar banu mikol am, v'rom'manu mikol lashon, v'kid'shanu b'mitsvotav, vatiten lanu Adonai Eloheynu b'ahava (on Shabat: Shabatot lim'nukha u) moadim l'simkha, khagim uzmanim l'sason, et yom (on Shabat: haShabat hazeh, v'et yom) khag hamatsot hazeh, zman kherutenu, (on Shabat: b'ahava,) mikra kodesh, zekher liy'tsiat Mitsrayim, ki vanu vakharta v'otanu kidashta mikol haamim, (on Shabat: v'Shabat) umoadey kodsh'kha (on Shabat: b'ahava uv'ratson,) b'simkha uvsason hinkhaltanu, barukh ata Adonai, m'kadesh (on Shabat: haShabat v')Yisrael v'hazmanim.

10 **בָּרוּךְ** אַתָּה יְיָ, אֱלֹהֵינוּ מֶלֶךְ הָעוֹלָם, אֲשֶׁר בָּחַר

11 בָּנוּ מִכָּל־עָם, וְרוֹמְמָנוּ מִכָּל־לָשׁוֹן, וְקִדְּשָׁנוּ

12 בְּמִצְוֹתָיו, וַתִּתֶּן־לָנוּ יְיָ אֱלֹהֵינוּ בְּאַהֲבָה (בשבת:

13 שַׁבָּתוֹת לִמְנוּחָה וּ)מוֹעֲדִים לְשִׂמְחָה, חַגִּים

14 וּזְמַנִּים לְשָׂשׂוֹן. אֶת־יוֹם (בשבת: הַשַּׁבָּת הַזֶּה,

15 וְאֶת־יוֹם) חַג הַמַּצּוֹת הַזֶּה. זְמַן חֵרוּתֵנוּ, (בשבת:

16 בְּאַהֲבָה,) מִקְרָא קֹדֶשׁ, זֵכֶר לִיצִיאַת מִצְרָיִם. כִּי

17 בָנוּ בָחַרְתָּ וְאוֹתָנוּ קִדַּשְׁתָּ מִכָּל־הָעַמִּים, (בשבת:

18 וְשַׁבָּת) וּמוֹעֲדֵי קָדְשֶׁךָ (בשבת: בְּאַהֲבָה וּבְרָצוֹן,)

19 בְּשִׂמְחָה וּבְשָׂשׂוֹן הִנְחַלְתָּנוּ. בָּרוּךְ אַתָּה יְיָ,

20 מְקַדֵּשׁ (בשבת: הַשַּׁבָּת וְ)יִשְׂרָאֵל וְהַזְּמַנִּים:

KADESH

RECITATION OF THE KIDDUSH

The first cup of wine is poured.

THE FIRST CUP

On Friday night, begin with the following paragraph:

And it was evening and it was morning.

1 **The sixth day.** The heavens, the earth, and all their hosts were finished. On the seventh day, God declared complete the work which He had done, and He rested on the seventh day from all His work which He had done. And God blessed the seventh day and made it holy, because on it He rested from all His work which He had done in creation.

Other nights of the week, begin here:

8 **Praised are You,** Eternal our God, Ruler of the universe, Creator of the fruit of the vine.

On Shabbat add the words in parentheses:

10 **Praised are You,** Eternal our God, Ruler of the universe, Who chose us from all peoples and exalted us among all nations, by making us holy with His commandments. With love You gave us (the Sabbath for rest, and) the festivals for happiness, holidays and seasons for rejoicing; as this day (of Sabbath, and this day) of the Feast of Matzoth, the season of our freedom, which is a holy assembly, in remembrance of the going out from Egypt. For you have chosen us from all peoples to make us holy with (the Sabbath and) Your holy festivals (with love and favor) in joy and in happiness. **Praised are You**, Who makes holy (the Sabbath and) Israel and the festive seasons.

On Saturday night add the following two blessings:

1 **Barukh ata Adonai**, Eloheynu Melekh Haolam, borey m'orey haesh.

בָּרוּךְ אַתָּה יְיָ, אֱלֹהֵינוּ מֶלֶךְ הָעוֹלָם, בּוֹרֵא 1
מְאוֹרֵי הָאֵשׁ: 2

3 **Barukh ata Adonai**, Eloheynu Melekh Haolam, hamavdil beyn kodesh l'khol, beyn or l'khoshekh, beyn Yisrael laamim, beyn yom hash'vii l'sheshet y'mey hamaase, beyn k'dushat Shabat lik'dushat yom tov hivdalta, v'et yom hash'vii misheshet y'mey hamaase kidashta, hivdalta v'kidashta et amekha Yisrael bikdushatekha, barukh ata Adonai, hamavdil beyn kodesh l'kodesh.

בָּרוּךְ אַתָּה יְיָ, אֱלֹהֵינוּ מֶלֶךְ הָעוֹלָם, הַמַּבְדִּיל 3
בֵּין קֹדֶשׁ לְחֹל, בֵּין אוֹר לְחֹשֶׁךְ, בֵּין יִשְׂרָאֵל 4
לָעַמִּים, בֵּין יוֹם הַשְּׁבִיעִי לְשֵׁשֶׁת יְמֵי הַמַּעֲשֶׂה. 5
בֵּין קְדֻשַּׁת שַׁבָּת לִקְדֻשַּׁת יוֹם טוֹב הִבְדַּלְתָּ. 6
וְאֶת־יוֹם הַשְּׁבִיעִי מִשֵּׁשֶׁת יְמֵי הַמַּעֲשֶׂה קִדַּשְׁתָּ. 7
הִבְדַּלְתָּ וְקִדַּשְׁתָּ אֶת־עַמְּךָ יִשְׂרָאֵל בִּקְדֻשָּׁתֶךָ. 8
בָּרוּךְ אַתָּה יְיָ, הַמַּבְדִּיל בֵּין קֹדֶשׁ לְקֹדֶשׁ: 9

10 **Barukh ata Adonai**, Eloheynu Melekh Haolam, shehekheyanu v'kiymanu v'higianu laz'man hazeh.

בָּרוּךְ אַתָּה יְיָ, אֱלֹהֵינוּ מֶלֶךְ הָעוֹלָם, שֶׁהֶחֱיָנוּ 10
וְקִיְּמָנוּ וְהִגִּיעָנוּ לַזְּמַן הַזֶּה: 11

Drink the first cup of wine while reclining on the left.

URCHATZ וּרְחַץ

WASHING THE HANDS

Hands are washed without reciting the blessing.

On Saturday night add the following two blessings:

1 Praised are You, Eternal our God, Ruler of the universe, creator of light and fire.

3 Praised are You, Eternal our God, Ruler of the universe, Who makes a distinction between the holy and the plain, between light and darkness, between Israel and the other nations, between the seventh day and the six days of work. You have made a distinction between the holiness of the Sabbath and the holiness of the festivals, and You made the seventh day holier than the six days of work. You have distinguished and made holy Your people Israel with Your holiness. Praised are You, Who makes a distinction between holiness and holiness.

10 Praised are You, Eternal our God, Ruler of the universe, who has given us life and sustenance and brought us to this happy season.

Drink the first cup of wine while reclining on the left.

URCHATZ

WASHING THE HANDS

Hands are washed without reciting the blessing.

כַּרְפַּס KARPAS

EATING A GREEN VEGETABLE

Take less than a kezayit (the volume of one olive) of the
karpas, dip it into salt water or vinegar, and recite the
following blessing, keeping in mind that it is also for the
bitter herbs (of maror and korekh), to be eaten later on:

1 **Barukh ata Adonai,** Eloheynu Melekh
Haolam, borey pri haadama.

1 בָּרוּךְ אַתָּה יְיָ, אֱלֹהֵינוּ מֶלֶךְ הָעוֹלָם, בּוֹרֵא פְּרִי
2 הָאֲדָמָה:

יַחַץ YACHATZ

BREAK THE MIDDLE MATZAH
AND HIDE HALF FOR THE AFIKOMAN

*The Leader of the Seder breaks the middle Matzah on the
plate, and leaving half of it there, puts aside the other half
until after the meal, for the Afikoman.*

מַגִּיד MAGID

THE PASSOVER STORY

Uncover the matzah and lift up the plate for all to see. The
recital of the Haggadah begins with the following words:

3 **Ha lakhma anya,** di akhalu avhatana
b'ara d'Mitsrayim, kol dikhfin yeytey
v'yeykhol, kol ditsrikh yeytey v'yifsakh,
hashata hakha, lashana habaa b'ara
d'Yisrael, hashata avdey, lashana habaa
b'ney khorin.

3 הָא לַחְמָא עַנְיָא, דִי אֲכָלוּ אַבְהָתָנָא בְּאַרְעָא
4 דְמִצְרָיִם. כָּל דִכְפִין יֵיתֵי וְיֵיכוֹל, כָּל דִצְרִיךְ יֵיתֵי
5 וְיִפְסַח. הָשַׁתָּא הָכָא, לְשָׁנָה הַבָּאָה בְּאַרְעָא
6 דְיִשְׂרָאֵל. הָשַׁתָּא עַבְדֵי, לְשָׁנָה הַבָּאָה בְּנֵי
7 חוֹרִין:

KARPAS

EATING A GREEN VEGETABLE

Take less than a kezayit (the volume of one olive) of the karpas, dip it into salt water or vinegar, and recite the following blessing, keeping in mind that it is also for the bitter herbs (of maror and korekh) to be eaten later on:

1 Praised are You, Eternal our God, Ruler of the universe, Creator of the fruit of the earth.

YACHATZ

BREAK THE MIDDLE MATZAH AND HIDE HALF FOR THE AFIKOMAN

The Leader of the Seder breaks the middle Matzah on the plate, and leaving half of it there, puts aside the other half until after the meal, for the Afikoman.

MAGID

THE PASSOVER STORY

Uncover the matzah and lift up the plate for all to see. The recital of the Haggadah begins with the following words:

3 This is the bread of affliction which our forefathers ate in the land of Egypt. All who are hungry – let them come and eat. All who are needy – let them come and celebrate the Passover with us. Now we are here; next year may we be in the Land of Israel. Now we are slaves; next year may we be free.

Put down the plate, cover the matzot, and pour the second
cup of wine. The youngest present asks the Four Questions.

THE FOUR QUESTIONS

**Ma nishtana halayla hazeh
mikol haleylot?**

מַה נִּשְׁתַּנָּה הַלַּיְלָה הַזֶּה מִכָּל הַלֵּילוֹת?

1 Sheb'khol haleylot anu okh'lin khamets umatsa, halayla hazeh kulo matsa.

1 שֶׁבְּכָל הַלֵּילוֹת אָנוּ אוֹכְלִין חָמֵץ וּמַצָּה, הַלַּיְלָה הַזֶּה כֻּלּוֹ מַצָּה:

2 Sheb'khol haleylot anu okh'lin sh'ar y'rakot, halayla hazeh maror.

2 שֶׁבְּכָל הַלֵּילוֹת אָנוּ אוֹכְלִין שְׁאָר יְרָקוֹת, הַלַּיְלָה הַזֶּה מָרוֹר:

3 Sheb'khol haleylot eyn anu matbilin afilu paam ekhat, halayla hazeh shtey f'amim.

3 שֶׁבְּכָל הַלֵּילוֹת אֵין אָנוּ מַטְבִּילִין אֲפִלּוּ פַּעַם אֶחָת, הַלַּיְלָה הַזֶּה שְׁתֵּי פְעָמִים:

4 Sheb'khol haleylot anu okh'lin beyn yosh'vin uveyn m'subin, halayla hazeh kulanu m'subin.

4 שֶׁבְּכָל הַלֵּילוֹת אָנוּ אוֹכְלִין בֵּין יוֹשְׁבִין וּבֵין מְסֻבִּין, הַלַּיְלָה הַזֶּה כֻּלָּנוּ מְסֻבִּין:

Restore the tray to its place and uncover the matzot
during the recitation of the Haggadah.

THE ANSWER

Avadim hayinu l'faro b'Mitsrayim, vayotsienu Adonai Eloheynu misham, b'yad khazaka uvizroa n'tuya, v'ilu lo hotsi Hakadosh Barukh Hu et avoteynu miMitsrayim, harey anu uvaneynu uv'ney vaneynu, m'shubadim hayinu l'faro b'Mitsrayim, vaafilu kulanu khakhamim, kulanu n'vonim, kulanu zkenim, kulanu yodim et hatora mitsva aleynu l'saper biy'tsiat Mitsrayim, v'khol hamarbe l'saper biy'tsiat Mitsrayim, harey ze m'shubakh.

5 עֲבָדִים הָיִינוּ לְפַרְעֹה בְּמִצְרָיִם. וַיּוֹצִיאֵנוּ יְיָ
6 אֱלֹהֵינוּ מִשָּׁם, בְּיָד חֲזָקָה וּבִזְרֹעַ נְטוּיָה. וְאִלּוּ
7 לֹא הוֹצִיא הַקָּדוֹשׁ בָּרוּךְ הוּא אֶת־אֲבוֹתֵינוּ
8 מִמִּצְרַיִם, הֲרֵי אָנוּ וּבָנֵינוּ וּבְנֵי בָנֵינוּ, מְשֻׁעְבָּדִים
9 הָיִינוּ לְפַרְעֹה בְּמִצְרָיִם. וַאֲפִלּוּ כֻּלָּנוּ חֲכָמִים,
10 כֻּלָּנוּ נְבוֹנִים, כֻּלָּנוּ זְקֵנִים, כֻּלָּנוּ יוֹדְעִים אֶת־
11 הַתּוֹרָה מִצְוָה עָלֵינוּ לְסַפֵּר בִּיצִיאַת מִצְרָיִם.
12 וְכָל הַמַּרְבֶּה לְסַפֵּר בִּיצִיאַת מִצְרָיִם, הֲרֵי זֶה
13 מְשֻׁבָּח:

14

Put down the plate, cover the matzot, and pour the second
cup of wine. The youngest present asks the Four Questions.

THE FOUR QUESTIONS

WHY IS THIS NIGHT DIFFERENT
FROM ALL OTHER NIGHTS?

1 On all other nights we eat either leavened bread or (matzah)
unleavened; on this night why only unleavened bread?

2 On all other nights we eat herbs of any kind on this night
why only bitter herbs?

3 On all other nights we do not dip our herbs even once; on
this night why do we dip them twice?

4 On all other nights we eat our meals in any manner; on this
night why do we sit around the table in a reclining position?

Restore the tray to its place and uncover the matzot
during the recitation of the Haggadah.

THE ANSWER

5 **We were slaves** of Pharaoh in Egypt and the Eternal our
God brought us out from there with a strong hand and
an outstretched arm. Now if God had not brought out our
forefathers from Egypt, then even we, our children, and
our children's children might still have been enslaved to
Pharaoh in Egypt. Therefore, even if we were all wise, all
men of understanding, and even if we were all old and well
learned in the Torah, it would still be our duty to tell the story
of the departure from Egypt. And the more one tells of the
departure from Egypt, the more is one to be praised.

1 **Maase** b'rabi Eliezer v'rabi Y'hoshua v'rabi Elazar ben Azarya v'rabi Akiva v'rabi Tarfon, shehayu m'subin Biv'ney Brak, v'hayu m'saprim biy'tsiat Mitsrayim kol oto halayla, ad shebau talmideyhem v'amru lahem. Raboteynu, higia zman kriat shma shel shakharit.

1	מַעֲשֶׂה בְּרַבִּי אֱלִיעֶזֶר וְרַבִּי יְהוֹשֻׁעַ וְרַבִּי אֶלְעָזָר
2	בֶּן־עֲזַרְיָה וְרַבִּי עֲקִיבָא וְרַבִּי טַרְפוֹן, שֶׁהָיוּ
3	מְסֻבִּין בִּבְנֵי־בְרַק, וְהָיוּ מְסַפְּרִים בִּיצִיאַת
4	מִצְרַיִם כָּל־אוֹתוֹ הַלַּיְלָה, עַד שֶׁבָּאוּ תַלְמִידֵיהֶם
5	וְאָמְרוּ לָהֶם: רַבּוֹתֵינוּ, הִגִּיעַ זְמַן קְרִיאַת שְׁמַע
6	שֶׁל שַׁחֲרִית:

7 **Amar Rabi Elazar** ben Azarya. Harey ani k'ven shivim shana, v'lo zakhiti sheteamer y'tsiat Mitsrayim baleylot, ad shedrasha ben zoma, sheneemar. L'maan tizkor et yom tseytkha meerets Mitsrayim kol y'mey khayekha, y'mey khayekha hayamim, kol y'mey khayekha, haleylot, vakhakhamim omrim. Y'mey khayekha, Haolam hazeh, kol y'mey khayekha, l'havi liy'mot hamashiakh.

7	אָמַר רַבִּי אֶלְעָזָר בֶּן־עֲזַרְיָה: הֲרֵי אֲנִי כְּבֶן
8	שִׁבְעִים שָׁנָה, וְלֹא זָכִיתִי שֶׁתֵּאָמֵר יְצִיאַת
9	מִצְרַיִם בַּלֵּילוֹת, עַד שֶׁדְּרָשָׁה בֶּן־זוֹמָא. שֶׁנֶּאֱמַר:
10	לְמַעַן תִּזְכֹּר אֶת יוֹם צֵאתְךָ מֵאֶרֶץ מִצְרַיִם
11	כֹּל יְמֵי חַיֶּיךָ. יְמֵי חַיֶּיךָ הַיָּמִים. כֹּל יְמֵי חַיֶּיךָ,
12	הַלֵּילוֹת. וַחֲכָמִים אוֹמְרִים: יְמֵי חַיֶּיךָ, הָעוֹלָם
13	הַזֶּה. כֹּל יְמֵי חַיֶּיךָ, לְהָבִיא לִימוֹת הַמָּשִׁיחַ:

4 **Barukh hamakom**, barukh hu, barukh shenatan tora l'amo Yisrael, barukh hu, k'neged arbaa vanim dibra tora. Ekhad khakham, v'ekhad rasha, v'ekhad tam, v'ekhad sheeyno yodeya lishol.

14	בָּרוּךְ הַמָּקוֹם, בָּרוּךְ הוּא. בָּרוּךְ שֶׁנָּתַן תּוֹרָה
15	לְעַמּוֹ יִשְׂרָאֵל, בָּרוּךְ הוּא. כְּנֶגֶד אַרְבָּעָה בָנִים
16	דִּבְּרָה תוֹרָה: אֶחָד חָכָם, וְאֶחָד רָשָׁע, וְאֶחָד
17	תָם, וְאֶחָד שֶׁאֵינוֹ יוֹדֵעַ לִשְׁאֹל:

3 **Khakham** ma hu omer? Ma haedot v'hakhukim v'hamishpatim, asher tsiva Adonai Eloheynu etkhem? V'af ata emar lo k'hilkhot hapesakh. Eyn maftirin akhar hapesakh afikoman.

18	חָכָם מַה הוּא אוֹמֵר? מָה הָעֵדֹת וְהַחֻקִּים
19	וְהַמִּשְׁפָּטִים, אֲשֶׁר צִוָּה יְיָ אֱלֹהֵינוּ אֶתְכֶם? וְאַף
20	אַתָּה אֱמָר־לוֹ כְּהִלְכוֹת הַפֶּסַח: אֵין מַפְטִירִין
21	אַחַר הַפֶּסַח אֲפִיקוֹמָן:

1 **It is told** that Rabbi Eliezer, Rabbi Joshua, Rabbi Elazar the son of Azariah, Rabbi Akiba, and Rabbi Tarfon sat all night in Bene-Berak telling the story of the departure from Egypt. Toward morning their students came to tell them that it was time for the morning prayers.

7 **Rabbi Elazar** the son of Azariah said: Here I am a man of seventy years, yet I did not understand why the story of the departure from Egypt should be told at night, until Ben Zoma explained it. The Bible commands us, saying "That you may remember the day of your going out from Egypt all the days of your life." Ben Zoma explained: The *days of your life* might mean only the days; *all the days of your life* includes the nights also. The other sages, however, explain it this way: The *days of your life* refers to this world only, but *all the days of your life* includes also the time of the Messiah.

14 **Praised is God,** Who gave the Torah to His people Israel. Praised is He. The Torah speaks about four sons: one who is wise and one who is contrary; one who is simple and one who does not even know how to ask a question.

18 **The wise son** asks: "What is the meaning of the rules, laws, and customs which the Eternal our God has commanded us?" You shall explain to him all the laws of Passover, to the very last detail about the afikoman.

	Transliteration	Hebrew	
1	**Rasha** ma hu omer? Ma haavoda hazot lakhem? Lakhem v'lo lo, ul'fi shehotsi et atsmo min haklal, kafar baikar, v'af ata hakhey et shinav, veemar lo. Baavur ze, asa Adonai li, b'tseyti miMitsrayim, li v'lo lo, ilu haya sham, lo haya nigal.	רָשָׁע מַה הוּא אוֹמֵר? מָה הָעֲבֹדָה הַזֹּאת לָכֶם? לָכֶם וְלֹא לוֹ. וּלְפִי שֶׁהוֹצִיא אֶת־עַצְמוֹ מִן הַכְּלָל, כָּפַר בָּעִקָּר. וְאַף אַתָּה הַקְהֵה אֶת־שִׁנָּיו, וֶאֱמָר־ לוֹ: בַּעֲבוּר זֶה, עָשָׂה יְיָ לִי, בְּצֵאתִי מִמִּצְרַיִם, לִי וְלֹא־לוֹ. אִלּוּ הָיָה שָׁם, לֹא הָיָה נִגְאָל:	1 2 3 4 5
6	**Tam** ma hu omer? Ma zot? V'amarta elav. B'khozek yad hotsianu Adonai miMitsrayim mibeyt avadim.	תָּם מַה הוּא אוֹמֵר? מַה זֹּאת? וְאָמַרְתָּ אֵלָיו: בְּחֹזֶק יָד הוֹצִיאָנוּ יְיָ מִמִּצְרַיִם מִבֵּית עֲבָדִים:	6 7
8	**V'sheeyno yodea lish'ol,** at p'takh lo, sheneemar. V'higadta l'vinkha, bayom hahu leymor. Baavur ze asa Adonai li, b'tseyti miMitsrayim.	וְשֶׁאֵינוֹ יוֹדֵעַ לִשְׁאוֹל, אַתְּ פְּתַח לוֹ. שֶׁנֶּאֱמַר: וְהִגַּדְתָּ לְבִנְךָ, בַּיּוֹם הַהוּא לֵאמֹר: בַּעֲבוּר זֶה עָשָׂה יְיָ לִי, בְּצֵאתִי מִמִּצְרָיִם:	8 9 10
1	**Yakhol merosh khodesh,** talmud lomar. Bayom hahu, e bayom hahu, yakhol mibod yom, talmud lomar. Baavur ze, baavur ze lo amarti, ela b'shaa sheyesh matsa umaror munakhim l'fanekha.	יָכוֹל מֵרֹאשׁ חֹדֶשׁ, תַּלְמוּד לוֹמַר: בַּיּוֹם הַהוּא. אִי בַּיּוֹם הַהוּא, יָכוֹל מִבְּעוֹד יוֹם, תַּלְמוּד לוֹמַר: בַּעֲבוּר זֶה. בַּעֲבוּר זֶה לֹא אָמַרְתִּי, אֶלָּא בְּשָׁעָה שֶׁיֵּשׁ מַצָּה וּמָרוֹר מֻנָּחִים לְפָנֶיךָ:	11 12 13 14
5	**Mitkhila** ovdey avoda zara hayu avoteynu, v'akhshav kervanu hamakom laavodato, sheneemar. Vayomer Y'hoshua el kol haam, ko amar Adonai Elohey Yisrael, b'ever hanahar yashvu avoteykhem meolam, Terakh avi Avraham vaavi Nakhor, vayaavdu elohim akherim. Vaekakh et avikhem et Avraham meever hanahar, vaolekh oto b'khol erets k'naan, vaarbe et zaro, vaeten lo et Yitzkak. Vaeten l'Yitskhak et Yaakov v'et Esav, vaeten l'Esav et har seir, lareshet oto, v'Yaakov uvanav yardu Mitsrayim.	מִתְּחִלָּה עוֹבְדֵי עֲבוֹדָה זָרָה הָיוּ אֲבוֹתֵינוּ, וְעַכְשָׁו קֵרְבָנוּ הַמָּקוֹם לַעֲבֹדָתוֹ. שֶׁנֶּאֱמַר: וַיֹּאמֶר יְהוֹשֻׁעַ אֶל־כָּל־הָעָם. כֹּה אָמַר יְיָ אֱלֹהֵי יִשְׂרָאֵל, בְּעֵבֶר הַנָּהָר יָשְׁבוּ אֲבוֹתֵיכֶם מֵעוֹלָם, תֶּרַח אֲבִי אַבְרָהָם וַאֲבִי נָחוֹר, וַיַּעַבְדוּ אֱלֹהִים אֲחֵרִים: וָאֶקַּח אֶת־אֲבִיכֶם אֶת־אַבְרָהָם מֵעֵבֶר הַנָּהָר, וָאוֹלֵךְ אוֹתוֹ בְּכָל־אֶרֶץ כְּנָעַן. וָאַרְבֶּה אֶת־ זַרְעוֹ, וָאֶתֶּן לוֹ אֶת־יִצְחָק: וָאֶתֵּן לְיִצְחָק אֶת־ יַעֲקֹב וְאֶת־עֵשָׂו. וָאֶתֵּן לְעֵשָׂו אֶת־הַר שֵׂעִיר, לָרֶשֶׁת אוֹתוֹ. וְיַעֲקֹב וּבָנָיו יָרְדוּ מִצְרָיִם:	15 16 17 18 19 20 21 22 23 24

1 **The contrary son** asks: "What is the meaning of this service to you?" Saying *you*, he excludes himself, and because he excludes himself from the group, he denies a basic principle. You may therefore tell him plainly: "Because of what the Eternal did for me when I came forth from Egypt," I do this. For *me* and not for *him*; had he been there, he would not have been redeemed.

6 **The simple son** asks: "What is this?" To him you shall say: "With a strong hand the Eternal brought us out of Egypt, from the house of bondage."

8 **As for the son who does not even know how to ask** a question, you must begin for him, as it is written in the Bible, "You shall tell your child on that day: This is done because of that which the Eternal did for me when I came forth out of Egypt."

11 **One might think** that the Seder ceremony should be performed on the first day of Nisan. The Torah therefore tells us "on that day" – on Passover. Saying "on that day," one might suppose that the Seder should be conducted during the daytime. But inasmuch as the Torah adds "because of all *this,*" I learn from it that the ceremony does not begin until the time when unleavened bread (matzah) and the bitter herbs are set before you – on Passover night.

15 **Long, long ago** our forefathers were worshippers of idols. Now the Eternal is our God and we worship Him. Even as the Bible tells us: "And Joshua said to all the people: Thus said the Eternal God of Israel: In days of old your forefathers lived beyond the river; that is Terah the father of Abraham and Nahor. They worshipped other gods. Then I took Abraham, your father, from beyond the river. I led him through the whole land of Canaan. Then I increased his family by giving him a son, Isaac. And I gave to Isaac two sons, Jacob and Esau. To Esau I gave Mount Seir as a possession, but Jacob and his sons went down to Egypt."

1 **Barukh** shomer havtakhato l'Yisrael, barukh hu, sheHakadosh Barukh Hu khishav et hakets, laasot k'ma sheamar l'Avraham Avinu bivrit beyn hab'tarim, sheneemar. Vayomer l'Avram, yadoa teda ki ger yihye zarakha b'erets lo lahem vaavadum, v'inu otam arba meot shana v'gam et hagoy asher yaavodu dan anokhi, v'akharey khen yetsu bir'khush gadol.

1 בָּרוּךְ שׁוֹמֵר הַבְטָחָתוֹ לְיִשְׂרָאֵל, בָּרוּךְ הוּא.
2 שֶׁהַקָּדוֹשׁ בָּרוּךְ הוּא חִשַּׁב אֶת־הַקֵּץ, לַעֲשׂוֹת
3 כְּמָה שֶׁאָמַר לְאַבְרָהָם אָבִינוּ בִּבְרִית בֵּין
4 הַבְּתָרִים, שֶׁנֶּאֱמַר: וַיֹּאמֶר לְאַבְרָם, יָדֹעַ תֵּדַע
5 כִּי־גֵר יִהְיֶה זַרְעֲךָ בְּאֶרֶץ לֹא לָהֶם וַעֲבָדוּם, וְעִנּוּ
6 אֹתָם אַרְבַּע מֵאוֹת שָׁנָה: וְגַם אֶת־הַגּוֹי אֲשֶׁר
7 יַעֲבֹדוּ דָן אָנֹכִי, וְאַחֲרֵי כֵן יֵצְאוּ בִּרְכֻשׁ גָּדוֹל:

Cover the matzot and raise the wine cup:

8 **V'hi sheamda** laavoteynu v'lanu, shelo ekhad bilvad, amad aleynu l'khalotenu, ela sheb'khol dor vador, omdim aleynu l'khalotenu, v'Hakadosh Barukh Hu matsilenu miyadam.

8 וְהִיא שֶׁעָמְדָה לַאֲבוֹתֵינוּ וְלָנוּ. שֶׁלֹּא אֶחָד
9 בִּלְבָד, עָמַד עָלֵינוּ לְכַלּוֹתֵנוּ, אֶלָּא שֶׁבְּכָל דּוֹר
10 וָדוֹר, עוֹמְדִים עָלֵינוּ לְכַלּוֹתֵנוּ. וְהַקָּדוֹשׁ בָּרוּךְ
11 הוּא מַצִּילֵנוּ מִיָּדָם:

Put down the wine cup and uncover the matzot:

2 **Tsey ulmad**, ma bikesh Lavan haarami laasot l'Yaakov Avinu, sheparo lo gazar ela al hazkharim, v'Lavan bikesh laakor et hakol, sheneemar. Arami oved avi, vayered Mitsraima, vayagor sham bi-m'tey m'at, vay'hi sham l'goy gadol atsum varav.

12 צֵא וּלְמַד, מַה בִּקֵּשׁ לָבָן הָאֲרַמִּי לַעֲשׂוֹת
13 לְיַעֲקֹב אָבִינוּ. שֶׁפַּרְעֹה לֹא גָזַר אֶלָּא עַל
14 הַזְּכָרִים, וְלָבָן בִּקֵּשׁ לַעֲקֹר אֶת־הַכֹּל. שֶׁנֶּאֱמַר:
15 אֲרַמִּי אֹבֵד אָבִי, וַיֵּרֶד מִצְרַיְמָה, וַיָּגָר שָׁם בִּמְתֵי
16 מְעָט. וַיְהִי שָׁם לְגוֹי גָּדוֹל עָצוּם וָרָב:

7 **Vayered Mitsraima**, anus al pi hadibur, vayagor sham, m'lamed shelo yarad Yaakov Avinu l'hishtakeya b'Mitsrayim, ela lagur sham, sheneemar. Vayomru el paro, lagur baarets banu, ki eyn mire latson asher laavadekha, ki khaved haraav b'erets k'naan, v'ata, yeshvu na avadekha b'erets Goshen.

17 וַיֵּרֶד מִצְרַיְמָה, אָנוּס עַל פִּי הַדִּבּוּר. וַיָּגָר
18 שָׁם, מְלַמֵּד שֶׁלֹּא יָרַד יַעֲקֹב אָבִינוּ לְהִשְׁתַּקֵּעַ
19 בְּמִצְרַיִם, אֶלָּא לָגוּר שָׁם, שֶׁנֶּאֱמַר: וַיֹּאמְרוּ אֶל־
20 פַּרְעֹה, לָגוּר בָּאָרֶץ בָּאנוּ, כִּי אֵין מִרְעֶה לַצֹּאן
21 אֲשֶׁר לַעֲבָדֶיךָ, כִּי כָבֵד הָרָעָב בְּאֶרֶץ כְּנָעַן.
22 וְעַתָּה, יֵשְׁבוּ־נָא עֲבָדֶיךָ בְּאֶרֶץ גֹּשֶׁן:

1 **Praised is God,** Who keeps His promise to Israel, praised be He. For God foretold the end of the bondage to Abraham at the Covenant of Sacrifices. For God said to Abraham: "Know you that your children will be strangers in a land not their own. They will be enslaved there and will be oppressed four hundred years. The nation who will oppress them shall, however, be judged. Afterward they will come forth with great wealth."

Cover the matzot and raise the wine cup:

8 **This promise** made to our forefathers holds true also for us. For more than once have they risen against us to destroy us; in every generation they rise against us and seek our destruction. But the holy One, blessed be He, saves us from their hands.

Put down the wine cup and uncover the matzot:

12 **Come and learn** what Laban the Syrian tried to do to our father Jacob. While Pharaoh decreed only against the males, Laban desired to uproot all. For so it is written: "A Syrian sought to destroy my father; and he went down to Egypt and dwelled there, a handful, few in number. There he became a nation, great, mighty, and numerous."

17 **"He went down to Egypt"** – why did he go down to Egypt? He was compelled by God's decree.

"He dwelled there" – this means that Jacob our father did not go down to Egypt to settle there but only to stay for short while; for so it is said, "And they said to Pharaoh, we have come to dwell in the land because there is no pasture for the flocks of your servants, since the famine is very bad in the land of Canaan; and now let your servants dwell in the land of Goshen."

1	**Bim'tey m'at**, k'ma sheneemar. B'shivim nefesh, yardu avotekha Mitsraima, v'ata, samkha Adonai Elohekha, k'khokhvey hashamayim larov.	בְּמְתֵי מְעָט, כְּמָה שֶׁנֶּאֱמַר: בְּשִׁבְעִים נֶפֶשׁ, יָרְדוּ אֲבֹתֶיךָ מִצְרָיְמָה. וְעַתָּה, שָׂמְךָ יְיָ אֱלֹהֶיךָ, כְּכוֹכְבֵי הַשָּׁמַיִם לָרֹב.

1
2
3

4	**Vay'hi sham** l'goy, m'lamed shehayu Yisrael m'tsuyanim sham.	וַיְהִי שָׁם לְגוֹי, מְלַמֵּד שֶׁהָיוּ יִשְׂרָאֵל מְצֻיָּנִים שָׁם:

4
5

6	**Gadol atsum**, k'ma sheneemar. uv'ney Yisrael, paru vayishr'tsu, vayirbu vayaatsmu bim'od m'od, vatimaley haarets otam.	גָּדוֹל עָצוּם, כְּמָה שֶׁנֶּאֱמַר: וּבְנֵי יִשְׂרָאֵל, פָּרוּ וַיִּשְׁרְצוּ, וַיִּרְבּוּ וַיַּעַצְמוּ בִּמְאֹד מְאֹד, וַתִּמָּלֵא הָאָרֶץ אֹתָם:

6
7
8

9	**Varav**, k'ma sheneemar. R'vava k'tsemakh hasade n'tatikh, vatirbi, vatigdli, vatavoi baadi adayim. Shadayim nakhonu, us'arekh tsimeyakh, v'at eyrom v'erya. Vaeevor alayikh vaerekh mitboseset b'damayikh, vaomar lakh b'damayikh khayi, vaomar lakh b'damayikh khayi.	וָרָב, כְּמָה שֶׁנֶּאֱמַר: רְבָבָה כְּצֶמַח הַשָּׂדֶה נְתַתִּיךְ, וַתִּרְבִּי, וַתִּגְדְּלִי, וַתָּבֹאִי בַּעֲדִי עֲדָיִים: שָׁדַיִם נָכֹנוּ, וּשְׂעָרֵךְ צִמֵּחַ, וְאַתְּ עֵרֹם וְעֶרְיָה: וָאֶעֱבֹר עָלַיִךְ וָאֶרְאֵךְ מִתְבּוֹסֶסֶת בְּדָמָיִךְ, וָאֹמַר לָךְ בְּדָמַיִךְ חֲיִי, וָאֹמַר לָךְ בְּדָמַיִךְ חֲיִי:

9
10
11
12
13

14	**Vayareu** otanu hamitsrim vayananu, vayitnu aleynu avoda kasha.	וַיָּרֵעוּ אֹתָנוּ הַמִּצְרִים וַיְעַנּוּנוּ, וַיִּתְּנוּ עָלֵינוּ עֲבֹדָה קָשָׁה:

14
15

16	**Vayareu** otanu hamitsrim, k'ma sheneemar. Hava nitkhakma lo, pen yirbe, v'haya ki tikrena milkhama, v'nosaf gam hu al soneynu, v'nilkham banu v'ala min haarets.	וַיָּרֵעוּ אֹתָנוּ הַמִּצְרִים, כְּמָה שֶׁנֶּאֱמַר: הָבָה נִתְחַכְּמָה לוֹ. פֶּן־יִרְבֶּה, וְהָיָה כִּי־תִקְרֶאנָה מִלְחָמָה, וְנוֹסַף גַּם הוּא עַל־שֹׂנְאֵינוּ, וְנִלְחַם־בָּנוּ וְעָלָה מִן־הָאָרֶץ:

16
17
18
19

20	**Vayananu**, k'ma sheneemar. Vayasimu alav sarey misim, l'maan anoto b'sivlotam. Vayiven arey misk'not l'faro, et pitom v'et raamses.	וַיְעַנּוּנוּ. כְּמָה שֶׁנֶּאֱמַר: וַיָּשִׂימוּ עָלָיו שָׂרֵי מִסִּים, לְמַעַן עַנֹּתוֹ בְּסִבְלֹתָם: וַיִּבֶן עָרֵי מִסְכְּנוֹת לְפַרְעֹה, אֶת־פִּתֹם וְאֶת־רַעַמְסֵס:

20
21
22

1 **"Few in number"** – as it is said: "Your forefathers went down into Egypt with seventy persons. Now the Eternal your God has made you as numerous as the stars in heaven."

4 **"And there he became a nation"** – from this we learn that Israel became a distinct nation in Egypt.

6 **"Great and mighty"** – as it is said: "And the children of Israel were fruitful and increased and multiplied and became very strong and numerous, so that the land was full of them."

9 **"And numerous"** – as it is said: "I have increased you as the growth of the field and you have become numerous and grown big and reached to excellence in beauty. You are fully grown, yet you remained naked and bare."

14 **"And the Egyptians** did evil to us and they made us suffer. They set upon us hard work."

16 **"And the Egyptians did evil to us"** – as it is said in the Bible: "Come, let us deal craftily with them, lest they increase yet more, and it may be that when war occurs they will be added to our enemies and fight against us and go up out of the land."

20 **"And they made us suffer"** – as the Bible relates: "So the Egyptians set taskmasters over them in order to oppress them with their burdens; and they built Pithom and Raamses as store cities for Pharaoh."

Vayitnu aleynu avoda kasha, k'ma sheneemar. vayaavidu Mitsrayim et b'ney Yisrael b'farekh.	1 **וַיִּתְּנוּ** עָלֵינוּ עֲבֹדָה קָשָׁה, כְּמָה שֶׁנֶּאֱמַר: וַיַּעֲבִדוּ 2 מִצְרַיִם אֶת־בְּנֵי יִשְׂרָאֵל בְּפָרֶךְ:
Vanitsak el Adonai Elohey avoteynu, vayishma Adonai et kolenu, vayar et anyenu, v'et amalenu, v'et lakhatsenu.	3 **וַנִּצְעַק** אֶל־יְיָ אֱלֹהֵי אֲבֹתֵינוּ, וַיִּשְׁמַע יְיָ אֶת־ 4 קֹלֵנוּ, וַיַּרְא אֶת־עָנְיֵנוּ, וְאֶת־עֲמָלֵנוּ, וְאֶת 5 לַחֲצֵנוּ:
Vanitsak el Adonai Elohey avoteynu, k'ma sheneemar. Vay'hi vayamim harabim hahem, vayamat Melekh Mitsrayim, vayeankhu v'ney Yisrael min haavoda vayizaku, vataal shavatam el haElohim min haavoda.	6 **וַנִּצְעַק** אֶל־יְיָ אֱלֹהֵי אֲבֹתֵינוּ, כְּמָה שֶׁנֶּאֱמַר: 7 וַיְהִי בַיָּמִים הָרַבִּים הָהֵם, וַיָּמָת מֶלֶךְ מִצְרַיִם, 8 וַיֵּאָנְחוּ בְנֵי־יִשְׂרָאֵל מִן־הָעֲבֹדָה וַיִּזְעָקוּ. וַתַּעַל 9 שַׁוְעָתָם אֶל־הָאֱלֹהִים מִן־הָעֲבֹדָה:
Vayishma Adonai et kolenu, k'ma she-neemar. Vayishma Elohim et naakatam, vayizkor Elohim et b'rito, et Avraham, et Yitskhak, v'et Yaakov.	10 **וַיִּשְׁמַע** יְיָ אֶת־קֹלֵנוּ, כְּמָה שֶׁנֶּאֱמַר: וַיִּשְׁמַע 11 אֱלֹהִים אֶת־נַאֲקָתָם, וַיִּזְכֹּר אֱלֹהִים אֶת־בְּרִיתוֹ, 12 אֶת־אַבְרָהָם, אֶת־יִצְחָק, וְאֶת יַעֲקֹב:
Vayar et anyenu, zo prishut derekh erets, k'ma sheneemar. Vayar Elohim et b'ney Yisrael, vayeda Elohim.	13 **וַיַּרְא** אֶת־עָנְיֵנוּ. זוֹ פְּרִישׁוּת דֶּרֶךְ אֶרֶץ. כְּמָה 14 שֶׁנֶּאֱמַר: וַיַּרְא אֱלֹהִים אֶת־בְּנֵי יִשְׂרָאֵל, וַיֵּדַע 15 אֱלֹהִים:
V'et amalenu, elu habanim, k'ma she-neemar. Kol haben hayilod hayora tashlikhuhu, v'khol habat t'khayun.	16 **וְאֶת־עֲמָלֵנוּ.** אֵלּוּ הַבָּנִים. כְּמָה שֶׁנֶּאֱמַר: 17 כָּל־הַבֵּן הַיִּלּוֹד הַיְאֹרָה תַּשְׁלִיכֻהוּ, וְכָל־הַבַּת 18 תְּחַיּוּן:
V'et lakhatsenu, ze hadkhak, k'ma sheneemar. v'gam raiti et halakhats, asher Mitsrayim lokhatsim otam.	19 **וְאֶת לַחֲצֵנוּ.** זֶה הַדְּחַק. כְּמָה שֶׁנֶּאֱמַר: וְגַם־ 20 רָאִיתִי אֶת־הַלַּחַץ, אֲשֶׁר מִצְרַיִם לֹחֲצִים אֹתָם:

1 **"And they set upon us hard work"** – as the Bible states: "And Egypt made the children of Israel labor rigorously."

3 **"So we cried to the Eternal**, the God of our ancestors, and the Eternal heard our voice, and He saw our affliction, and our burden, and our oppression."

6 **"So we cried unto the Eternal**, the God of our ancestors" as the Bible recounts: "And it came to pass in the course of those many days that the King of Egypt died and the children of Israel moaned because of servitude and cried out, and their outcry from servitude came up unto God."

10 **"And the Eternal heard our voice"** – as the Bible tells: "And God heard their groaning, and God remembered His covenant with Abraham, with Isaac, and with Jacob."

13 **"And He saw our affliction"** – this phrase suggests the enforced separation of husband and wife under Pharaoh's persecution, as it is written: "And God saw the children of Israel and God understood their plight."

16 **"And our burden"** – this recalls the drowning of the male children, as it is said: "Every son that is born you shall cast into the Nile, but every daughter you may keep alive."

19 **"And our oppression"** – this refers to crushing our lives, as the Bible says: "And I have seen the oppression with which the Egyptians are oppressing them."

1	**Vayotsienu** Adonai miMitsrayim, b'yad khazaka, uvizroa n'tuya, uvmora gadol uvotot uvmoftim.	וַיּוֹצִאֵנוּ יְיָ מִמִּצְרַיִם, בְּיָד חֲזָקָה, וּבִזְרֹעַ נְטוּיָה, וּבְמֹרָא גָּדוֹל וּבְאֹתוֹת וּבְמוֹפְתִים:	1 2
3	**Vayotsienu** Adonai miMitsrayim, lo al y'dey malakh, v'lo al y'dey saraf, v'lo al y'dey shaliakh, ela Hakadosh Barukh Hu bikhvodo uvatsmo, sheneemar. V'avarti v'erets Mitsrayim balayla hazeh, v'hikeyti khol b'khor b'erets Mitsrayim, meadam v'ad b'hema, uv'khol Elohey Mitsrayim eese shfatim ani Adonai.	וַיּוֹצִאֵנוּ יְיָ מִמִּצְרַיִם. לֹא עַל־יְדֵי מַלְאָךְ, וְלֹא עַל־יְדֵי שָׂרָף, וְלֹא עַל־יְדֵי שָׁלִיחַ, אֶלָּא הַקָּדוֹשׁ בָּרוּךְ הוּא בִּכְבוֹדוֹ וּבְעַצְמוֹ. שֶׁנֶּאֱמַר: וְעָבַרְתִּי בְאֶרֶץ מִצְרַיִם בַּלַּיְלָה הַזֶּה, וְהִכֵּיתִי כָל־בְּכוֹר בְּאֶרֶץ מִצְרַיִם, מֵאָדָם וְעַד בְּהֵמָה, וּבְכָל־אֱלֹהֵי מִצְרַיִם אֶעֱשֶׂה שְׁפָטִים אֲנִי יְיָ:	3 4 5 6 7 8
9	**V'avarti** v'erets Mitsrayim balayla hazeh, ani v'lo malakh, v'hikeyti khol b'khor b'erets Mitsrayim, ani v'lo saraf, uv'khol Elohey Mitsrayim eese shfatim, ani v'lo hashaliakh, ani Adonai, ani hu v'lo akher.	וְעָבַרְתִּי בְאֶרֶץ־מִצְרַיִם בַּלַּיְלָה הַזֶּה, אֲנִי וְלֹא מַלְאָךְ. וְהִכֵּיתִי כָל בְּכוֹר בְּאֶרֶץ־מִצְרַיִם, אֲנִי וְלֹא שָׂרָף, וּבְכָל־אֱלֹהֵי מִצְרַיִם אֶעֱשֶׂה שְׁפָטִים, אֲנִי וְלֹא הַשָּׁלִיחַ. אֲנִי יְיָ, אֲנִי הוּא וְלֹא אַחֵר:	9 10 11 12
	B'yad khazaka, zo hadever, k'ma sheneemar. Hiney yad Adonai hoya, b'mikn'kha asher basade, basusim bakhamorim bagmalim, babakar uvatson, dever kaved m'od.	בְּיָד חֲזָקָה. זוֹ הַדֶּבֶר, כְּמָה שֶׁנֶּאֱמַר: הִנֵּה יַד־יְיָ הוֹיָה, בְּמִקְנְךָ אֲשֶׁר בַּשָּׂדֶה, בַּסּוּסִים בַּחֲמֹרִים בַּגְּמַלִּים, בַּבָּקָר וּבַצֹּאן, דֶּבֶר כָּבֵד מְאֹד:	13 14 15
	Uvizroa n'tuya, zo hakherev, k'ma sheneemar. V'kharbo shlufa b'yado, n'tuya al Y'rushalayim.	וּבִזְרֹעַ נְטוּיָה. זוֹ הַחֶרֶב. כְּמָה שֶׁנֶּאֱמַר: וְחַרְבּוֹ שְׁלוּפָה בְּיָדוֹ, נְטוּיָה עַל־יְרוּשָׁלָיִם:	16 17
	Uvmora gadol, ze gilui shkhina, k'ma sheneemar. O hanisa Elohim, lavo lakakhat lo goy mikerev goy, b'masot b'otot uvmoftim uvmilkhama, uvyad khazaka uvizroa n'tuya, uvmoraiim g'dolim, k'khol asher asa lakhem Adonai Eloheykhem b'Mitsrayim, l'eynekha.	וּבְמוֹרָא גָּדוֹל. זֶה גִּלּוּי שְׁכִינָה, כְּמָה שֶׁנֶּאֱמַר: אוֹ הֲנִסָּה אֱלֹהִים, לָבוֹא לָקַחַת לוֹ גוֹי מִקֶּרֶב גּוֹי, בְּמַסֹּת בְּאֹתֹת וּבְמוֹפְתִים וּבְמִלְחָמָה, וּבְיָד חֲזָקָה וּבִזְרוֹעַ נְטוּיָה, וּבְמוֹרָאִים גְּדֹלִים. כְּכֹל אֲשֶׁר־עָשָׂה לָכֶם יְיָ אֱלֹהֵיכֶם בְּמִצְרַיִם, לְעֵינֶיךָ:	18 19 20 21 22 23

1 **"And the Eternal brought us forth** from Egypt, with a strong hand, and with an outstretched arm, and with great terror, and with signs and wonders."

3 **"And the Eternal brought us forth** from Egypt" – not by a ministering angel, not by a fiery angel, not by a messenger, but by Himself, in His glory, did the Holy One, blessed be He, as the Bible records: "And I will pass through the land of Egypt on that night, and I will smite all the firstborn in the land of Egypt from man to beast, and against all the gods of Egypt I will execute judgments. It is I, the Eternal."

9 **"And I will pass through** the land of Egypt" – I and not a ministering angel; "and I will smite the firstborn in the land of Egypt" – I and not a fiery angel; "and against all the gods of Egypt I will execute judgments" – I and not a messenger; "I the Eternal" – I and no other.

13 **"With a strong hand"** – this refers to the cattle plague, as it is said in the Bible: "Behold, the hand of the Eternal will be against the cattle that is in the field, against the horses, the donkeys, the camels, the oxen, and the sheep, a very grievous plague."

16 **"And with an outstretched arm"** – this refers to the sword, as the Bible states: "His sword drawn in His hand, outstretched against Jerusalem."

18 **"And with great terror"** – this refers to the Revelation of God to Israel, as it is said: "Has any god ever tried to go and remove one nation from the midst of another nation, with trials, with signs and wonders, and with battle, and with strong hand and outstretched arm, and with great terrors, as all that the Eternal your God did for you in Egypt before your eyes?"

1 **Uvotot**, ze hamate, k'ma sheneemar. V'et hamate hazeh tikakh b'yadekha, asher taase bo et haotot.

1 **וּבְאֹתוֹת.** זֶה הַמַּטֶּה, כְּמָה שֶׁנֶּאֱמַר: וְאֶת
2 הַמַּטֶּה הַזֶּה תִּקַּח בְּיָדֶךָ. אֲשֶׁר תַּעֲשֶׂה־בּוֹ אֶת
3 הָאֹתֹת:

4 **Uvmoftim**, ze hadam, k'ma sheneemar. V'natati moftim, bashamayim uvaarets.

4 **וּבְמוֹפְתִים.** זֶה הַדָּם, כְּמָה שֶׁנֶּאֱמַר: וְנָתַתִּי
5 מוֹפְתִים, בַּשָּׁמַיִם וּבָאָרֶץ:

Spill three drops of wine from the cup during the recitation
of the words "blood, and fire, and pillars of smoke."

6 **1 – DAM, 2 – VA'ESH,**
3 – V'TIMROT ASHAN.

6 1 – דָּם, 2 – וָאֵשׁ,
3 – וְתִימְרוֹת עָשָׁן:

7 **Davar akher.** B'yad khazaka shtayim, uvizroa n'tuya shtayim, uvmora gadol shtayim, uvotot shtayim, uvmoftim shtayim.

7 **דָּבָר אַחֵר:** בְּיָד חֲזָקָה שְׁתַּיִם. וּבִזְרֹעַ נְטוּיָה
8 שְׁתַּיִם. וּבְמוֹרָא גָּדוֹל שְׁתַּיִם. וּבְאֹתוֹת שְׁתַּיִם.
9 וּבְמֹפְתִים שְׁתַּיִם:

10 **Elu** eser makot shehevi Hakadosh Barukh Hu al hamitsrim b'Mitsrayim, v'elu hen.

10 **אֵלוּ** עֶשֶׂר מַכּוֹת שֶׁהֵבִיא הַקָּדוֹשׁ בָּרוּךְ הוּא
11 עַל־הַמִּצְרִים בְּמִצְרַיִם, וְאֵלוּ הֵן:

28

1 **"And with signs"** – this refers to the rod of Moses, as it is said: "And thou, Moses, shalt take in thy hand this rod wherewith thou shalt do the signs."

4 **"And wonders"** – this refers to the plague of blood, as is written in Scripture: "I will put wonders in heaven and on earth."

Spill three drops of wine from the cup during the recitation of the words "blood, and fire, and pillars of smoke."

6 **1 – BLOOD 2 – FIRE
3 – PILLARS OF SMOKE**

7 **Another interpretation is as follows:**

"With a strong hand" – refers to two plagues; "with an outstretched arm" – two; "with great terror" – two; "with signs" – two, and "with wonders" refers to two plagues. Thus we have the ten plagues that the Holy One, blessed be He, brought upon the Egyptians in Egypt; and they are as follows:

10 Thus we have the ten plauges that the Holy One, Praised be He, brought upon the Egyptians in Egypt; and they are as follows:

**Spill ten drops of wine from the cup during the
recitation of each of the ten plagues:**

5 – דֶּבֶר.   4 – עָרוֹב.   3 – כִּנִּים.   2 – צְפַרְדֵּעַ.   1 – דָּם.

DEVER   AROV   KINIM   TSFARDEYA   DAM

6 – שְׁחִין.   7 – בָּרָד.   8 – אַרְבֶּה.   9 – חֹשֶׁךְ.   10 – מַכַּת בְּכוֹרוֹת:

MAKAT B'KHOROT   KHOSHEKH   ARBEH   BARAD   SHKHIN

Spill ten drops of wine from the cup during the recitation of each of the ten plagues:

One

BLOOD   *DAM*

Two

FROGS   *TSFARDEYA*

Three

VERMIN   *KINIM*

Four

BEASTS   *AROV*

Five

CATTLE DISEASE   *DEVER*

Six

BOILS   *SHKHIN*

Seven

HAIL   *BARAD*

Eight

LOCUSTS   *ARBEH*

Nine

DARKNESS   *KHOSHEKH*

Ten

SLAYING OF THE FIRSTBORN
MAKAT B'KHOROT

Rabi Y'huda haya noten bahem simanim:	רַבִּי יְהוּדָה הָיָה נוֹתֵן בָּהֶם סִמָּנִים:	1

Spill three drops of wine:

D'TSAKH, ADASH, B'AKHAV.	דְּצַ"ךְ, עֲדַ"שׁ, בְּאַחַ"ב:	2

32

1 **Rabbi Judah** used to refer to the ten plagues by their Hebrew
initials –

Spill three drops of wine:

2 **D'TZAKH, ADASH, B'AKHAV**

1 Rabi Yosey Haglili omer. Minayin ata omer, shelaku hamitsrim b'Mitsrayim eser makot, v'al hayam laku khamishim makot? B'Mitsrayim ma hu omer. Vayomru hakhartumim el paro, etsba Elohim hi, v'al hayam ma hu omer? Vayar Yisrael et hayad hag'dola, asher asa Adonai b'Mitsrayim, vayiru haam et Adonai, vayaaminu bAdonai, uvMoshe avdo. Kama laku b'etsba? Eser makot, emor meata. B'Mitsrayim laku eser makot, v'al hayam laku khamishim makot.	1 **רַבִּי יוֹסֵי הַגְּלִילִי** אוֹמֵר: מִנַּיִן אַתָּה אוֹמֵר, 2 שֶׁלָּקוּ הַמִּצְרִים בְּמִצְרַיִם עֶשֶׂר מַכּוֹת, וְעַל הַיָּם 3 לָקוּ חֲמִשִּׁים מַכּוֹת? בְּמִצְרַיִם מַה הוּא אוֹמֵר: 4 וַיֹּאמְרוּ הַחַרְטֻמִּם אֶל־פַּרְעֹה, אֶצְבַּע אֱלֹהִים 5 הִיא. וְעַל הַיָּם מַה הוּא אוֹמֵר? וַיַּרְא יִשְׂרָאֵל 6 אֶת־הַיָּד הַגְּדֹלָה, אֲשֶׁר עָשָׂה יְיָ בְּמִצְרַיִם, 7 וַיִּירְאוּ הָעָם אֶת־יְיָ. וַיַּאֲמִינוּ בַּיְיָ, וּבְמֹשֶׁה 8 עַבְדּוֹ: כַּמָּה לָקוּ בָּאֶצְבַּע? עֶשֶׂר מַכּוֹת. אֱמוֹר 9 מֵעַתָּה: בְּמִצְרַיִם לָקוּ עֶשֶׂר מַכּוֹת, וְעַל־הַיָּם 10 לָקוּ חֲמִשִּׁים מַכּוֹת:
1 Rabi Eliezer omer. Minayin shekol maka umaka, shehevi Hakadosh Barukh Hu al hamitsrim b'Mitsrayim, haita shel arba makot? sheneemar. y'shalakh bam kharon apo, evra vazaam v'tsara, mishlakhat malakhey raim. Evra akhat, vazaam shtayim, v'tsara shalosh, mishlakhat malakhey raim arba, emor meata. B'Mitsrayim laku arbaim makot, v'al hayam laku matayim makot.	11 **רַבִּי אֱלִיעֶזֶר** אוֹמֵר: מִנַּיִן שֶׁכָּל־מַכָּה וּמַכָּה, 12 שֶׁהֵבִיא הַקָּדוֹשׁ בָּרוּךְ הוּא עַל הַמִּצְרִים 13 בְּמִצְרַיִם, הָיְתָה שֶׁל אַרְבַּע מַכּוֹת? שֶׁנֶּאֱמַר: 14 יְשַׁלַּח־בָּם חֲרוֹן אַפּוֹ, עֶבְרָה וָזַעַם וְצָרָה, 15 מִשְׁלַחַת מַלְאֲכֵי רָעִים: עֶבְרָה אַחַת. וָזַעַם 16 שְׁתַּיִם. וְצָרָה שָׁלשׁ. מִשְׁלַחַת מַלְאֲכֵי רָעִים 17 אַרְבַּע. אֱמֹר מֵעַתָּה: בְּמִצְרַיִם לָקוּ אַרְבָּעִים 18 מַכּוֹת, וְעַל הַיָּם לָקוּ מָאתַיִם מַכּוֹת:
Rabi Akiva omer. Minayin shekol maka umaka, shehevi Hakadosh Barukh Hu al hamitsrim b'Mitsrayim, haita shel khamesh makot? sheneemar. y'shalakh bam kharon apo, evra vazaam v'tsara, mishlakhat malakhey raim. Kharon apo akhat, evra shtayim, vazaam shalosh, v'tsara arba, mishlakhat malakhey raim khamesh, emor meata. B'Mitsrayim laku khamishim makot, v'al hayam laku khamishim umatayim makot.	19 **רַבִּי עֲקִיבָא** אוֹמֵר: מִנַּיִן שֶׁכָּל־מַכָּה וּמַכָּה, 20 שֶׁהֵבִיא הַקָּדוֹשׁ בָּרוּךְ הוּא עַל הַמִּצְרִים בְּמִצְרַיִם, 21 הָיְתָה שֶׁל חָמֵשׁ מַכּוֹת? שֶׁנֶּאֱמַר: יְשַׁלַּח־בָּם חֲרוֹן 22 אַפּוֹ, עֶבְרָה וָזַעַם וְצָרָה, מִשְׁלַחַת מַלְאֲכֵי רָעִים: 23 חֲרוֹן אַפּוֹ אַחַת. עֶבְרָה שְׁתַּיִם. וָזַעַם שָׁלשׁ. 24 וְצָרָה אַרְבַּע. מִשְׁלַחַת מַלְאֲכֵי רָעִים חָמֵשׁ. אֱמֹר 25 מֵעַתָּה: בְּמִצְרַיִם לָקוּ חֲמִשִּׁים מַכּוֹת, וְעַל הַיָּם 26 לָקוּ חֲמִשִּׁים וּמָאתַיִם מַכּוֹת.

1 **Rabbi Jose the Galilean** said: How can one show that following the ten plagues in Egypt itself the Egyptians were smitten with fifty plagues at the Red Sea? Of one of the plagues in Egypt it is said, "The soothsayers said to Pharaoh, the plague is the finger of God," while at the Red Sea it is said, "And Israel saw the strong hand which the Eternal had shown against Egypt, and the people revered the Eternal and believed in the Eternal and His servant Moses." If one finger of God in Egypt caused ten plagues, we may assume from this that the whole hand of God at the Red Sea would cause fifty plagues.

11 **Rabbi Eliezer** said: How can one show that every plague which the Holy One, praised be He, brought in Egypt upon the Egyptians was fourfold in character? For it is said: He sent against the Egyptians in His burning anger, Wrath, Indignation, Trouble, and the Messengers of Evil." This is to be interpreted that each plague descended with Wrath (1), Indignation (2), Trouble (3), and the sending of Messengers of Evil (4). If, then, the Egyptians in Egypt were stricken with ten fourfold plagues, making forty, then following the earlier interpretation, at the Red Sea they suffered two hundred plagues.

19 **Rabbi Akiba** said: In similar fashion you can show that every plague which the Holy One, praised be He, brought in Egypt upon the Egyptians was fivefold in character. Interpret the same verse to say, "He sent against the Egyptians His Burning Anger (1), Wrath (2), Indignation (3), Trouble (4), and the Messengers of Evil (5)." Thus, if the Egyptians in Egypt were stricken with ten fivefold plagues, making fifty, then at the Red Sea they suffered two hundred and fifty plagues.

Kama maalot tovot lamakom aleynu.	כַּמָּה מַעֲלוֹת טוֹבוֹת לַמָּקוֹם עָלֵינוּ:	1
Ilu hotsianu miMitsrayim, v'lo asa vahem shfatim, dayenu.	אִלּוּ הוֹצִיאָנוּ מִמִּצְרַיִם, וְלֹא עָשָׂה בָהֶם שְׁפָטִים, דַּיֵּנוּ:	2
Ilu asa vahem shfatim, v'lo asa vEyloheyhem, dayenu.	אִלּוּ עָשָׂה בָהֶם שְׁפָטִים, וְלֹא עָשָׂה בֵאלֹהֵיהֶם, דַּיֵּנוּ:	3
Ilu asa vEyloheyhem, v'lo harag et b'khoreyhem, dayenu.	אִלּוּ עָשָׂה בֵאלֹהֵיהֶם, וְלֹא הָרַג אֶת־בְּכוֹרֵיהֶם, דַּיֵּנוּ:	4
Ilu harag et b'khoreyhem, v'lo natan lanu et mamonam, dayenu.	אִלּוּ הָרַג אֶת־בְּכוֹרֵיהֶם, וְלֹא נָתַן לָנוּ אֶת־מָמוֹנָם, דַּיֵּנוּ:	5
Ilu natan lanu et mamonam, v'lo kara lanu et hayam, dayenu.	אִלּוּ נָתַן לָנוּ אֶת־מָמוֹנָם, וְלֹא קָרַע לָנוּ אֶת־הַיָּם, דַּיֵּנוּ:	6
Ilu kara lanu et hayam, v'lo heeviranu v'tokho bekharava, dayenu.	אִלּוּ קָרַע לָנוּ אֶת־הַיָּם, וְלֹא הֶעֱבִירָנוּ בְתוֹכוֹ בֶּחָרָבָה, דַּיֵּנוּ:	7
Ilu heeviranu b'tokho bekharava, v'lo shika tsareynu b'tokho, dayenu.	אִלּוּ הֶעֱבִירָנוּ בְתוֹכוֹ בֶּחָרָבָה, וְלֹא שִׁקַּע צָרֵינוּ בְּתוֹכוֹ, דַּיֵּנוּ:	8
Ilu shika tsareynu b'tokho, v'lo sipek tsorkenu bamidbar arbaim shana, dayenu.	אִלּוּ שִׁקַּע צָרֵינוּ בְּתוֹכוֹ, וְלֹא סִפֵּק צָרְכֵּנוּ בַּמִּדְבָּר אַרְבָּעִים שָׁנָה, דַּיֵּנוּ:	9
Ilu sipek tsarkenu bamidbar arbaim shana, v'lo heekhilanu et haman, dayenu.	אִלּוּ סִפֵּק צָרְכֵּנוּ בַּמִּדְבָּר אַרְבָּעִים שָׁנָה, וְלֹא הֶאֱכִילָנוּ אֶת־הַמָּן, דַּיֵּנוּ:	10
Ilu heekhilanu et haman, v'lo natan lanu et haShabat, dayenu.	אִלּוּ הֶאֱכִילָנוּ אֶת־הַמָּן, וְלֹא נָתַן לָנוּ אֶת־הַשַּׁבָּת, דַּיֵּנוּ:	11
Ilu natan lanu et haShabat, v'lo kervanu lifney har sinai, dayenu.	אִלּוּ נָתַן לָנוּ אֶת־הַשַּׁבָּת, וְלֹא קֵרְבָנוּ לִפְנֵי הַר סִינַי, דַּיֵּנוּ:	12
Ilu kervanu lifney har sinai, v'lo natan lanu et hatora, dayenu.	אִלּוּ קֵרְבָנוּ לִפְנֵי הַר סִינַי, וְלֹא נָתַן לָנוּ אֶת־הַתּוֹרָה, דַּיֵּנוּ:	13
Ilu natan lanu et hatora, v'lo hikhnisanu l'erets Yisrael, dayenu.	אִלּוּ נָתַן לָנוּ אֶת־הַתּוֹרָה, וְלֹא הִכְנִיסָנוּ לְאֶרֶץ יִשְׂרָאֵל, דַּיֵּנוּ:	14

1   How thankful must we be to God, the All-
    Present, for all the good He did for us.

2   Had He brought us out from Egypt
    And not executed judgment against them,
        It would have been enough for us!

3   Had He executed judgment against them
    And not done justice to their idols,
        It would have been enough for us!

4   Had He done justice to their idols
    And not slain their firstborn,
        It would have been enough for us!

5   Had He slain their firstborn
    And not given us their property,
        It would have been enough for us!

6   Had He given us their property
    And not divided the sea for us,
        It would have been enough for us!

7   Had He divided the sea for us
    And not brought us through it dry-shod,
        It would have been enough for us!

8   Had He brought us through it dry-shod
    And not drowned our oppressors in it,
        It would have been enough for us!

9   Had He drowned our oppressors in it
    And not helped us forty years in the desert,
        It would have been enough for us!

10 Had He helped us forty years in the desert
    And not fed us manna,
        It would have been enough for us!

11 Had He fed us manna
    And not given us the Sabbath,
        It would have been enough for us!

Continue on page 39

15	אִלּוּ הִכְנִיסָנוּ לְאֶרֶץ יִשְׂרָאֵל, וְלֹא בָנָה לָנוּ אֶת־בֵּית הַבְּחִירָה, דַּיֵּנוּ:	Ilu hikhnisanu l'erets Yisrael, v'lo vana lanu et beyt hab'khira, dayenu.

עַל אַחַת כַּמָּה וְכַמָּה טוֹבָה כְפוּלָה וּמְכֻפֶּלֶת לַמָּקוֹם עָלֵינוּ: שֶׁהוֹצִיאָנוּ מִמִּצְרַיִם, וְעָשָׂה בָהֶם שְׁפָטִים, וְעָשָׂה בֵאלֹהֵיהֶם, וְהָרַג אֶת־בְּכוֹרֵיהֶם, וְנָתַן לָנוּ אֶת־מָמוֹנָם, וְקָרַע לָנוּ אֶת־הַיָּם, וְהֶעֱבִירָנוּ בְתוֹכוֹ בֶּחָרָבָה, וְשִׁקַּע צָרֵינוּ בְּתוֹכוֹ, וְסִפֵּק צָרְכֵּנוּ בַּמִּדְבָּר אַרְבָּעִים שָׁנָה, וְהֶאֱכִילָנוּ אֶת־הַמָּן, וְנָתַן לָנוּ אֶת־הַשַּׁבָּת, וְקֵרְבָנוּ לִפְנֵי הַר סִינַי, וְנָתַן לָנוּ אֶת־הַתּוֹרָה, וְהִכְנִיסָנוּ לְאֶרֶץ יִשְׂרָאֵל, וּבָנָה לָנוּ אֶת־בֵּית הַבְּחִירָה, לְכַפֵּר עַל־כָּל־עֲוֹנוֹתֵינוּ.

Al akhat kama v'khama tova kh'fula umkhupelet lamakom aleynu. She-hotsianu miMitsrayim, v'asa vahem shfatim, v'asa vEyloheyhem, v'harag et b'khoreyhem, v'natan lanu et mamonam, v'kara lanu et hayam, v'heeviranu v'tokho bekharava, v'shika tsareynu b'tokho, v'sipek tsarkenu bamidbar arbaim shana, v'heekhilanu et haman, v'natan lanu et haShabat, v'kervanu lifney har sinai, v'natan lanu et hatora, v'hikhnisanu l'erets Yisrael, uvana lanu et beyt hab'khira, l'khaper al kol avonoteynu.

רַבָּן גַּמְלִיאֵל הָיָה אוֹמֵר: כָּל שֶׁלֹּא אָמַר שְׁלֹשָׁה דְבָרִים אֵלּוּ בַּפֶּסַח, לֹא יָצָא יְדֵי חוֹבָתוֹ, וְאֵלּוּ הֵן:

Raban Gamliel haya omer. Kol shelo amar shlosha d'varim elu bapesakh, lo yatsa y'dey khovato, v'elu hen.

פֶּסַח, מַצָּה, וּמָרוֹר:

Pesakh, matzah, umaror.

פֶּסַח שֶׁהָיוּ אֲבוֹתֵינוּ אוֹכְלִים, בִּזְמַן שֶׁבֵּית הַמִּקְדָּשׁ הָיָה קַיָּם, עַל שׁוּם מָה? עַל שׁוּם שֶׁפָּסַח הַקָּדוֹשׁ בָּרוּךְ הוּא, עַל בָּתֵּי אֲבוֹתֵינוּ בְּמִצְרַיִם, שֶׁנֶּאֱמַר: וַאֲמַרְתֶּם זֶבַח פֶּסַח הוּא לַיְיָ, אֲשֶׁר פָּסַח עַל בָּתֵּי בְנֵי יִשְׂרָאֵל בְּמִצְרַיִם בְּנָגְפּוֹ אֶת־מִצְרַיִם, וְאֶת־בָּתֵּינוּ הִצִּיל, וַיִּקֹּד הָעָם וַיִּשְׁתַּחֲווּ:

Pesakh shehayu avoteynu okhlim, bizman shebeyt hamikdash haya ka-yam, al shum ma? Al shum shepasakh HaKadosh Barukh Hu, al batey avoteynu b'Mitsrayim, sheneemar. Vaamartem zevakh pesakh hu lAdonai, asher pasakh al batey v'ney Yisrael b'Mitsrayim b'nagpo et Mitsrayim, v'et bateynu hitsil, vayikod haam vayishtakhavu.

12   Had He given us the Sabbath
And not brought us to Mount Sinai,
      It would have been enough for us!

13   Had He brought us to Mount Sinai
And not given us the Torah,
      It would have been enough for us!

14   Had He given us the Torah
And not brought us into the Land of Israel,
      It would have been enough for us!

15   Had He brought us to the Land of Israel
And not built for us the Holy Temple,
      It would have been enough for us!

---

1 **How much** more so do we have to be thankful for the manifold and unbounded blessings of the All-Present God: That He brought us out from Egypt, and executed judgment against them, and did justice to their idols, and slew their firstborn, and gave us their property, and divided the sea for us, and brought us through it dry-shod, and drowned our oppressors in it, and helped us for forty years in the desert, and fed us manna, and gave us the Sabbath, and brought us to Mount Sinai, and gave us the Torah, and brought us into the Land of Israel, and built for us the Holy Temple where we could atone for all our sins.

11 **Rabban Gamliel** used to say: Whoever does not explain the following three symbols at the Seder on Passover has not fulfilled his duty:

14   **THE PASSOVER OFFERING**
            THE MATZAH
            THE BITTER HERBS

15 **The Passover** offering which our fathers ate in Temple days, what was the reason for it? It was because the Holy One, blessed be He, passed over the houses of our forefathers in Egypt, as it is written in the Bible: "And you shall say it is

Continue on page 41

Raise the matzah and show it:

1 **Matsa** zo sheanu okhlim, al shum ma? Al shum shelo hispik b'tsekam shel avoteynu l'hakhamits, ad shenigla aleyhem Melekh malkhey ham'lakhim, Hakadosh Barukh Hu, ug'alam, sheneemar. Vayofu et habatsek asher hotsiu miMitsrayim, ugot matsot, ki lo khamets, ki gorshu miMitsrayim, v'lo yakhlu l'hitmameyha, v'gam tseyda lo asu lahem.

1 מַצָּה זוֹ שֶׁאָנוּ אוֹכְלִים, עַל שׁוּם מָה? עַל שׁוּם
2 שֶׁלֹּא הִסְפִּיק בְּצֵקָם שֶׁל אֲבוֹתֵינוּ לְהַחֲמִיץ, עַד
3 שֶׁנִּגְלָה עֲלֵיהֶם מֶלֶךְ מַלְכֵי הַמְּלָכִים, הַקָּדוֹשׁ
4 בָּרוּךְ הוּא, וּגְאָלָם, שֶׁנֶּאֱמַר: וַיֹּאפוּ אֶת־הַבָּצֵק
5 אֲשֶׁר הוֹצִיאוּ מִמִּצְרַיִם, עֻגֹת מַצּוֹת, כִּי לֹא
6 חָמֵץ, כִּי גֹרְשׁוּ מִמִּצְרַיִם, וְלֹא יָכְלוּ לְהִתְמַהְמֵהַּ,
7 וְגַם צֵדָה לֹא עָשׂוּ לָהֶם.

Point to the bitter herbs:

3 **Maror** ze sheanu okhlim, al shum ma? Al shum shemer'ru hamitsrim et kha-yey avoteynu b'Mitsrayim, sheneemar. Vay'mar'ru et khayeyhem baavoda kasha, b'khomer uvilvenim, uv'khol avoda basade, et kol avodatam, asher avdu vahem b'farekh.

8 מָרוֹר זֶה שֶׁאָנוּ אוֹכְלִים, עַל שׁוּם מָה? עַל שׁוּם
9 שֶׁמֵּרְרוּ הַמִּצְרִים אֶת־חַיֵּי אֲבוֹתֵינוּ בְּמִצְרַיִם,
10 שֶׁנֶּאֱמַר: וַיְמָרְרוּ אֶת־חַיֵּיהֶם בַּעֲבֹדָה קָשָׁה,
11 בְּחֹמֶר וּבִלְבֵנִים, וּבְכָל־עֲבֹדָה בַּשָּׂדֶה, אֶת כָּל־
12 עֲבֹדָתָם, אֲשֶׁר עָבְדוּ בָהֶם בְּפָרֶךְ.

B'khol dor vador khayav adam lirot et atsmo, k'ilu hu yatsa miMitsrayim, sheneemar. V'higadta l'vinkha bayom hahu leymor. Baavur ze asa Adonai li, b'tseyti miMitsrayim, lo et avoteynu bilvad, gaal Hakadosh Barukh Hu, ela af otanu gaal imahem, sheneemar. V'otanu hotsi misham, l'maan havi otanu, latet lanu et haarets asher nishba laavoteynu.

13 בְּכָל־דּוֹר וָדוֹר חַיָּב אָדָם לִרְאוֹת אֶת־עַצְמוֹ,
14 כְּאִלּוּ הוּא יָצָא מִמִּצְרַיִם, שֶׁנֶּאֱמַר: וְהִגַּדְתָּ
15 לְבִנְךָ בַּיּוֹם הַהוּא לֵאמֹר: בַּעֲבוּר זֶה עָשָׂה יְיָ
16 לִי, בְּצֵאתִי מִמִּצְרַיִם. לֹא אֶת־אֲבוֹתֵינוּ בִּלְבָד,
17 גָּאַל הַקָּדוֹשׁ בָּרוּךְ הוּא, אֶלָּא אַף אוֹתָנוּ גָּאַל
18 עִמָּהֶם, שֶׁנֶּאֱמַר: וְאוֹתָנוּ הוֹצִיא מִשָּׁם, לְמַעַן
19 הָבִיא אֹתָנוּ, לָתֶת לָנוּ אֶת־הָאָרֶץ אֲשֶׁר נִשְׁבַּע
20 לַאֲבֹתֵינוּ.

the Passover offering for the Eternal Who passed over the houses of the children of Israel in Egypt when He smote the Egyptians and spared our houses. And the people bowed their heads and worshipped."

Raise the matzah and show it:

1 **This matzah** which we eat, what is the reason for it? It is because there was not time for the dough of our ancestors in Egypt to become leavened, before the Ruler of all, the Holy One, praised be He, revealed Himself to them and redeemed them, as it is told in the Bible: "And the dough which they had brought out from Egypt they baked into cakes of unleavened bread, for it had not leavened, because they were thrust out of Egypt and they could not tarry, nor had they prepared for themselves any provisions.

Point to the bitter herbs:

8 **These bitter herbs** which we eat, what is their meaning? They are eaten to recall that the Egyptians embittered the lives of our forefathers in Egypt, as it is written: "And they embittered their lives with hard labor: with mortar and bricks, with every kind of work in the fields; all the work which they made them do was rigorous."

13 **In every** generation one must look upon himself as if he personally had come out from Egypt, as the Bible says: "And you shall tell your son on that day, saying, it is because of that which the Eternal did to me when I went forth from Egypt." For it was not only our ancestors whom the Holy One, praised be He, redeemed; He redeemed us too, with them, as it is said: "He brought us out from there that He might lead us to and give us the land which He pledged to our forefathers."

Cover the matzah and raise the cup of wine:

L'fikhakh anakhnu khayavim l'hodot, l'halel, l'shabeyakh, l'faer, l'romem, l'hader, l'varekh, l'aley ul'kales, l'mi sheasa laavoteynu v'lanu et kol hanisim haelu, hotsianu meavdut l'kherut, miyagon l'simkha, umeevel l'yom tov, umeafela l'or gadol, umishibud lig'ula, v'nomar l'fanav shira khadasha, hal'luya.	1 לְפִיכָךְ אֲנַחְנוּ חַיָּבִים לְהוֹדוֹת, לְהַלֵּל, לְשַׁבֵּחַ, 2 לְפָאֵר, לְרוֹמֵם, לְהַדֵּר, לְבָרֵךְ, לְעַלֵּה וּלְקַלֵּס, 3 לְמִי שֶׁעָשָׂה לַאֲבוֹתֵינוּ וְלָנוּ אֶת־כָּל־הַנִּסִּים 4 הָאֵלּוּ. הוֹצִיאָנוּ מֵעַבְדוּת לְחֵרוּת, מִיָּגוֹן 5 לְשִׂמְחָה, וּמֵאֵבֶל לְיוֹם טוֹב, וּמֵאֲפֵלָה לְאוֹר 6 גָּדוֹל, וּמִשִּׁעְבּוּד לִגְאֻלָּה. וְנֹאמַר לְפָנָיו שִׁירָה 7 חֲדָשָׁה. הַלְלוּיָהּ:

Put down the cup and continue:

Hal'luya, hal'lu avdey Adonai, hal'lu et shem Adonai. Y'hi shem Adonai m'vorakh, meata v'ad olam. Mimizrakh shemesh ad m'voo, m'hulal shem Adonai. Ram al kol goyim Adonai, al hashamayim k'vodo. Mi kAdonai Eloheynu, hamagbihi lashavet. hamashpili lirot, bashamayim uvaarets. M'kimi meafar dal, meashpot yarim evyon. L'hoshivi im n'divim, im n'divey amo. Moshivi akeret habayit, em habanim smekha, hal'luya.	8 הַלְלוּיָהּ. הַלְלוּ עַבְדֵי יְיָ, הַלְלוּ אֶת־שֵׁם יְיָ: יְהִי 9 שֵׁם יְיָ מְבֹרָךְ, מֵעַתָּה וְעַד עוֹלָם: מִמִּזְרַח שֶׁמֶשׁ 10 עַד מְבוֹאוֹ, מְהֻלָּל שֵׁם יְיָ: רָם עַל־כָּל־גּוֹיִם יְיָ, 11 עַל הַשָּׁמַיִם כְּבוֹדוֹ: מִי כַּייָ אֱלֹהֵינוּ, הַמַּגְבִּיהִי 12 לָשָׁבֶת: הַמַּשְׁפִּילִי לִרְאוֹת, בַּשָּׁמַיִם וּבָאָרֶץ: 13 מְקִימִי מֵעָפָר דָּל, מֵאַשְׁפֹּת יָרִים אֶבְיוֹן: 14 לְהוֹשִׁיבִי עִם־נְדִיבִים, עִם נְדִיבֵי עַמּוֹ: מוֹשִׁיבִי 15 עֲקֶרֶת הַבַּיִת, אֵם הַבָּנִים שְׂמֵחָה, הַלְלוּיָהּ:
B'tseyt Yisrael miMitsrayim, beyt Yaakov meam loez. Haita Y'huda l'kodsho, Yisrael mamshlotav. Hayam raa vayanos, haYarden yisov l'akhor. Heharim rakdu kh'eylim, gvaot kiv'ney tson. Ma l'kha hayam ki tanus, haYarden tisov l'akhor. Heharim tirk'du kh'eylim, gvaot kiv'ney tson. Milifney Adon khuli arets, milifney Eloha Yaakov. Hahofki hatsur agam mayim, khalamish l'mayno mayim.	16 בְּצֵאת יִשְׂרָאֵל מִמִּצְרָיִם, בֵּית יַעֲקֹב מֵעַם לֹעֵז: 17 הָיְתָה יְהוּדָה לְקָדְשׁוֹ, יִשְׂרָאֵל מַמְשְׁלוֹתָיו: 18 הַיָּם רָאָה וַיָּנֹס, הַיַּרְדֵּן יִסֹּב לְאָחוֹר: הֶהָרִים 19 רָקְדוּ כְאֵילִים, גְּבָעוֹת כִּבְנֵי־צֹאן: מַה־לְּךָ הַיָּם 20 כִּי תָנוּס, הַיַּרְדֵּן תִּסֹּב לְאָחוֹר: הֶהָרִים תִּרְקְדוּ 21 כְאֵילִים, גְּבָעוֹת כִּבְנֵי־צֹאן: מִלִּפְנֵי אָדוֹן חוּלִי 22 אָרֶץ, מִלִּפְנֵי אֱלוֹהַ יַעֲקֹב: הַהֹפְכִי הַצּוּר אֲגַם־ 23 מָיִם, חַלָּמִישׁ לְמַעְיְנוֹ־מָיִם.

Cover the matzah and raise the cup of wine:

1 **Therefore** it is our duty to thank and to praise in song and prayer, to glorify and extol Him Who performed all these wonders for our forefathers and for us. He brought us out from slavery to freedom, from anguish to joy, from sorrow to festivity, from darkness to great light. Let us therefore sing before Him a new song. Praise the Eternal.

Put down the cup and continue:

8 **Halleluyah** – Praise the Eternal. Praise, ye servants of the Eternal, praise the name of the Eternal. Blessed be the name of the Eternal from now and forevermore; from the rising of the sun to its going down. Praised be the name of the Eternal. Supreme above all nations is the Eternal; his glory is above the heavens. Who is like unto the Eternal our God, throned in exaltation, Who looks down to both the heavens and the earth? He raises up the poor from the dust, lifts up the needy from the ash-heap, to seat them with princes, with princes of His people; he makes the childless woman dwell in her household as a joyful mother of children. Halleluyah – praise the Eternal.

16 **When Israel** went forth from Egypt, the house of Jacob from a people of a strange tongue, Judah became his sanctuary, Israel his dominion. The sea beheld and fled, the Jordan turned back. The mountains skipped like rams, the hills, like lambs. O sea, what makes you run away? Jordan, that thou turnest back, you mountains, that you skip like rams, you hills, like lambs? Quake, earth, before the Eternal, At the presence of the God of Jacob, Who turns the rock into a pool of water, The flint into a fountain of water.

Raise the cup of wine and say:

1 | **Barukh ata** Adonai, Eloheynu Melekh Haolam, asher g'alanu v'gaal et avoteynu miMitsrayim, v'higianu lalayla hazeh, leekhal bo matsa umaror, ken, Adonai Eloheynu vEylohey avoteynu, yagienu l'moadim v'lirgalim akherim, habaim likratenu l'shalom, smekhim b'vinyan irekha, v'sasim baavodatekha, v'nokhal sham min hazvakhim umin hap'sakhim (on Motzei Shabat: min hap'sakhim umin hazvakhim), asher yagia damam al kir mizbakhakha l'ratson, v'node l'kha shir khadash, al g'ulatenu v'al p'dut nafshenu, barukh ata Adonai, gaal Yisrael.

1 בָּרוּךְ אַתָּה יְיָ, אֱלֹהֵינוּ מֶלֶךְ הָעוֹלָם, אֲשֶׁר
2 גְּאָלָנוּ וְגָאַל אֶת־אֲבוֹתֵינוּ מִמִּצְרַיִם, וְהִגִּיעָנוּ
3 לַלַּיְלָה הַזֶּה, לֶאֱכָל־בּוֹ מַצָּה וּמָרוֹר. כֵּן, יְיָ
4 אֱלֹהֵינוּ וֵאלֹהֵי אֲבוֹתֵינוּ, יַגִּיעֵנוּ לְמוֹעֲדִים
5 וְלִרְגָלִים אֲחֵרִים, הַבָּאִים לִקְרָאתֵנוּ לְשָׁלוֹם.
6 שְׂמֵחִים בְּבִנְיַן עִירֶךָ, וְשָׂשִׂים בַּעֲבוֹדָתֶךָ, וְנֹאכַל
7 שָׁם מִן הַזְּבָחִים וּמִן הַפְּסָחִים (במוצש״ק אומרים: מִן
8 הַפְּסָחִים וּמִן הַזְּבָחִים), אֲשֶׁר יַגִּיעַ דָּמָם עַל
9 קִיר מִזְבַּחֲךָ לְרָצוֹן, וְנוֹדֶה לְךָ שִׁיר חָדָשׁ, עַל
10 גְּאֻלָּתֵנוּ וְעַל פְּדוּת נַפְשֵׁנוּ. בָּרוּךְ אַתָּה יְיָ, גָּאַל
11 יִשְׂרָאֵל:

THE SECOND CUP

Barukh ata Adonai, Eloheynu Melekh Haolam, borey pri hagafen.

12 בָּרוּךְ אַתָּה יְיָ, אֱלֹהֵינוּ מֶלֶךְ הָעוֹלָם, בּוֹרֵא פְּרִי
13 הַגָּפֶן:

Drink the wine while reclining on the left.

רְחְצָה RACHTZAH

WASHING THE HANDS

The hands are washed followed by the recital of the following blessing:

Barukh ata Adonai, Eloheynu Melekh Haolam, asher kidshanu b'mitsvtav, v'tsivanu al n'tilat yadayim.

14 בָּרוּךְ אַתָּה יְיָ, אֱלֹהֵינוּ מֶלֶךְ הָעוֹלָם, אֲשֶׁר
15 קִדְּשָׁנוּ בְּמִצְוֹתָיו, וְצִוָּנוּ עַל נְטִילַת יָדָיִם:

Raise the cup of wine and say:

1 **Praised are You,** Eternal our God, Ruler of the universe, Who redeemed us and redeemed our forefathers from Egypt, and brought us to this night to eat thereon matzah and bitter herbs. Thus may the Eternal our God and God of our fathers bring us to future feasts and festivals in peace, and to the upbuilding of Your city Jerusalem, and to the happiness of Your service, so that we may partake there of the ancient offerings. We shall then offer to You a new song for our redemption and salvation. Praised are You, Eternal, Who redeemed Israel.

THE SECOND CUP

12 **Praised are You**, Eternal our God, Ruler of the universe, Creator of the fruit of the vine.

Drink the wine while reclining on the left.

RACHTZAH

WASHING THE HANDS

The hands are washed followed by the recital of the following blessing:

14 **Praised are You**, Eternal our God, Ruler of the universe, Who made us holy with His commandments and commanded us concerning the washing of the hands.

מוֹצִיא

MOTZI

Raise the remaining matzot and say the following blessing:

1 **Barukh** ata Adonai, Eloheynu Melekh Haolam, hamotsi lekhem min haarets.

1 בָּרוּךְ אַתָּה יְיָ, אֱלֹהֵינוּ מֶלֶךְ הָעוֹלָם, הַמּוֹצִיא
2 לֶחֶם מִן הָאָרֶץ:

מַצָּה

MATZAH

Put down the bottom matzah and recite the following blessing over the broken matzah and the top one. (Keep in mind that this blessing also applies to the korekh, which will be with the third matzah and the eating of the afikoman.)

3 **Barukh** ata Adonai, Eloheynu Melekh Haolam, asher kidshanu b'mitsvtav v'tsivanu al akhilat matsa.

3 בָּרוּךְ אַתָּה יְיָ, אֱלֹהֵינוּ מֶלֶךְ הָעוֹלָם, אֲשֶׁר
4 קִדְּשָׁנוּ בְּמִצְוֹתָיו וְצִוָּנוּ עַל אֲכִילַת מַצָּה:

Eat a kezayit (the volume of one olive) of each of the two matzot while reclining on the left.

מָרוֹר MAROR

BITTER HERBS

Take a kezayit of the maror and dip it into the haroset. (Keep in mind that this blessing also applies to the maror eaten with the korekh.)

5 **Barukh** ata Adonai, Eloheynu Melekh Haolam, asher kidshanu b'mitsvtav v'tsivanu al akhilat maror.

5 בָּרוּךְ אַתָּה יְיָ, אֱלֹהֵינוּ מֶלֶךְ הָעוֹלָם, אֲשֶׁר
6 קִדְּשָׁנוּ בְּמִצְוֹתָיו וְצִוָּנוּ עַל אֲכִילַת מָרוֹר:

MOTZI

Raise the remaining matzot and say the following blessing:

1 Praised are You, Eternal our God, Ruler of the universe, Who brings forth bread from the earth.

MATZAH

Put down the bottom matzah and recite the following blessing over the broken matzah and the top one. (Keep in mind that this blessing also applies to the korekh, which will be with the third matzah and the eating of the afikoman.)

3 Praised are You, Eternal our God, Ruler of the universe, Who made us holy with His commandments and commanded us to eat matzah.

Eat a kezayit (the volume of one olive) of each of the two matzot while reclining on the left.

MAROR

BITTER HERBS

Take a kezayit of the maror and dip it into the haroset. (Keep in mind that this blessing also applies to the maror eaten with the korekh.)

5 Praised are You, Eternal our God, Ruler of the universe, Who made us holy with His commandments and commanded us concerning the eating of bitter herbs.

כּוֹרֵךְ KORECH

EATING THE BITTER HERBS AND MATZAH TOGETHER

**Combine a kezayit of the third matzah and a
kezayit of the maror like a sandwich.**

1 **Zekher** lamikdash k'Hilel. Ken asa Hilel
bizman shebeyt hamikdash haya kayam, haya
korekh pesakh matsa umaror v'okhel b'yakhad,
l'kayem ma sheneemar. Al matsot um'rorim
yokhluhu.

1 **זֵכֶר** לַמִּקְדָּשׁ כְּהִלֵּל: כֵּן עָשָׂה הִלֵּל בִּזְמַן
2 שֶׁבֵּית הַמִּקְדָּשׁ הָיָה קַיָּם. הָיָה כּוֹרֵךְ פֶּסַח
3 מַצָּה וּמָרוֹר וְאוֹכֵל בְּיַחַד, לְקַיֵּם מַה שֶׁנֶּאֱמַר:
4 עַל־מַצּוֹת וּמְרוֹרִים יֹאכְלֻהוּ:

שֻׁלְחָן עוֹרֵךְ SHULCHAN ORECH

THE FESTIVE MEAL

**Eat a festive meal. It is permitted to drink wine between
the second and third cups. Many have the custom of
beginning the meal with eggs dipped in salt water.**

צָפוּן TZAFUN

AFTER THE MEAL, THE AFIKOMAN IS DISTRIBUTED TO ALL

**After the meal, take the afikoman and divide it among all the members
of the household. Eat it in the reclining position. One does not eat
or drink after the afikoman, except for the required cups of wine.**

KORECH

EATING THE BITTER HERBS AND MATZAH TOGETHER

Combine a kezayit of the third matzah and a kezayit of the maror like a sandwich.

1 **In remembrance** of the holy Temple, we do as Hillel did in Temple times: He put matzah and bitter herbs together and ate them as a sandwich, in order to observe literally the words of the Torah: "They shall eat it (the Passover offering) with matzah and bitter herbs."

SHULCHAN ORECH

THE FESTIVE MEAL

Eat a festive meal. It is permitted to drink wine between the second and third cups. Many have the custom of beginning the meal with eggs dipped in salt water.

TZAFUN

AFTER THE MEAL, THE AFIKOMAN IS DISTRIBUTED TO ALL

After the meal, take the afikoman and divide it among all the members of the household. Eat it in the reclining position. One does not eat or drink after the afikoman, except for the required cups of wine.

בָּרֵךְ BARECH

GRACE AFTER THE MEAL

1
Shir hamaalot, b'shuv Adonai et shivat tsiyon hayinu k'kholmim. Az yimaley skhok pinu ulshonenu rina, az yomru vagoyim higdil Adonai laasot im ele. Higdil Adonai laasot imanu hayinu smekhim. Shuva Adonai et shvitenu kaafikim banegev. Hazorim b'dima b'rina yiktsoru. Halokh yelekh uvakho nosey meshekh hazara, bo yavo v'rina nosey alumotav.

1 שִׁיר הַמַּעֲלוֹת, בְּשׁוּב יְיָ אֶת שִׁיבַת צִיּוֹן הָיִינוּ
2 כְּחֹלְמִים: אָז יִמָּלֵא שְׂחוֹק פִּינוּ וּלְשׁוֹנֵנוּ רִנָּה,
3 אָז יֹאמְרוּ בַגּוֹיִם הִגְדִּיל יְיָ לַעֲשׂוֹת עִם אֵלֶּה:
4 הִגְדִּיל יְיָ לַעֲשׂוֹת עִמָּנוּ הָיִינוּ שְׂמֵחִים: שׁוּבָה יְיָ
5 אֶת שְׁבִיתֵנוּ כַּאֲפִיקִים בַּנֶּגֶב: הַזֹּרְעִים בְּדִמְעָה
6 בְּרִנָּה יִקְצֹרוּ: הָלוֹךְ יֵלֵךְ וּבָכֹה נֹשֵׂא מֶשֶׁךְ הַזָּרַע,
7 בֹּא יָבֹא בְרִנָּה נֹשֵׂא אֲלֻמֹּתָיו:

**When the zimmun is said, begin here. If a minyan
is present, the phrase "Eloheynu" is added.**

The Leader:

8
Rabotai/gvirotai/khaverai n'varekh

8 רַבּוֹתַי/גְּבִירוֹתַי/חֲבֵרַי נְבָרֵךְ!

The others respond:

9
Y'hi shem Adonai m'vorakh meata v'ad olam.

9 יְהִי שֵׁם יְיָ מְבֹרָךְ מֵעַתָּה וְעַד עוֹלָם.

The Leader repeats the response and continues:
Insert the appropriate phrases:

Bir'shut/baal habayit/baalat habayit/ maranan/rabanan/rabotai khaverai, n'varekh (Eloheynu) sheakhalnu mishelo.

10 בִּרְשׁוּת בַּעַל הַבַּיִת/בַּעֲלַת הַבַּיִת/מָרָנָן/רַבָּנָן/
11 רַבּוֹתַי/חֲבֵרַי, נְבָרֵךְ (בעשרה אֱלֹהֵינוּ) שֶׁאָכַלְנוּ
12 מִשֶּׁלּוֹ.

The others respond:

Barukh (Eloheynu) sheakhalnu mishelo uvtuvo khayinu.

13 בָּרוּךְ (בעשרה אֱלֹהֵינוּ) שֶׁאָכַלְנוּ מִשֶּׁלּוֹ וּבְטוּבוֹ
14 חָיִינוּ.

The Leader repeats the response above and all continue.

BARECH

GRACE AFTER THE MEAL

1 **A Pilgrim Song** when the Eternal brought the exiles back to Zion we were as in a dream. Our mouth was filled with laughter and our tongue with song. The nations said: The Eternal has done great things for them. Yes, the Eternal did great things for us and we are very happy. Restore our good fortune, O Eternal, as dry streams that flow again. They that sow in tears shall reap in joy. Though the planter may weep as He carries seed to the field, he will yet return with joy, bearing the sheaves of grain.

When the zimmun is said, begin here. If a minyan
is present, the phrase "our God" is added.

The Leader:

8 Let us say grace.

The others respond:

9 May the name of the Eternal be blessed from now and for-evermore.

The Leader repeats the response and continues:
Insert the appropriate phrases:

10 With the permission of all present, let us praise Him [our God] Whose food we have eaten.

The others respond:

13 **Praised is our God**, Whose food we have eaten and in Whose goodness we live.

The Leader repeats the response above and all continue.

1 | **Barukh** ata Adonai, Eloheynu Melekh Haolam, hazan et Haolam kulo b'tuvo b'khen b'khesed uvrakhamim, hu noten lekhem l'khol basar, ki l'olam khasdo, uvtuvo hagadol tamid lo khasar lanu, v'al yekhsar lanu mazon l'olam vaed, baavur shmo hagadol, ki hu el zan um'farnes lakol, umetiv lakol, umekhin mazon l'khol b'riyotav asher bara (kaamur. Poteyakh et yadekha, umasbia l'khol khai ratson), barukh ata Adonai, hazan et hakol.

1 בָּרוּךְ אַתָּה יְיָ, אֱלֹהֵינוּ מֶלֶךְ הָעוֹלָם, הַזָּן אֶת
2 הָעוֹלָם כֻּלּוֹ בְּטוּבוֹ בְּחֵן בְּחֶסֶד וּבְרַחֲמִים, הוּא
3 נוֹתֵן לֶחֶם לְכָל בָּשָׂר, כִּי לְעוֹלָם חַסְדּוֹ. וּבְטוּבוֹ
4 הַגָּדוֹל תָּמִיד לֹא חָסַר לָנוּ, וְאַל יֶחְסַר לָנוּ מָזוֹן
5 לְעוֹלָם וָעֶד. בַּעֲבוּר שְׁמוֹ הַגָּדוֹל, כִּי הוּא אֵל
6 זָן וּמְפַרְנֵס לַכֹּל, וּמֵטִיב לַכֹּל, וּמֵכִין מָזוֹן לְכָל
7 בְּרִיּוֹתָיו אֲשֶׁר בָּרָא (כָּאָמוּר: פּוֹתֵחַ אֶת יָדֶךָ,
8 וּמַשְׂבִּיעַ לְכָל חַי רָצוֹן). בָּרוּךְ אַתָּה יְיָ, הַזָּן אֶת
9 הַכֹּל:

Node l'kha Adonai Eloheynu al she-hinkhalta laavoteynu, erets khemda tova ur'khava, v'al shehotseytanu Adonai Eloheynu meerets Mitsrayim, ufditanu mibeyt avadim, v'al b'ritkha shekhatamta bivsarenu, v'al toratkha shelimadtanu, v'al khukekha shehodatanu, v'al khayim khen vakhesed shekhonantanu, v'al akhilat mazon shaata zan um'farnes otanu tamid, b'khol yom uv'khol et uv'khol shaa.

10 נוֹדֶה לְךָ יְיָ אֱלֹהֵינוּ עַל שֶׁהִנְחַלְתָּ לַאֲבוֹתֵינוּ,
11 אֶרֶץ חֶמְדָּה טוֹבָה וּרְחָבָה, וְעַל שֶׁהוֹצֵאתָנוּ יְיָ
12 אֱלֹהֵינוּ מֵאֶרֶץ מִצְרַיִם, וּפְדִיתָנוּ מִבֵּית עֲבָדִים,
13 וְעַל בְּרִיתְךָ שֶׁחָתַמְתָּ בִּבְשָׂרֵנוּ, וְעַל תּוֹרָתְךָ
14 שֶׁלִּמַּדְתָּנוּ, וְעַל חֻקֶּיךָ שֶׁהוֹדַעְתָּנוּ, וְעַל חַיִּים
15 חֵן וָחֶסֶד שֶׁחוֹנַנְתָּנוּ, וְעַל אֲכִילַת מָזוֹן שָׁאַתָּה
16 זָן וּמְפַרְנֵס אוֹתָנוּ תָּמִיד, בְּכָל יוֹם וּבְכָל עֵת
17 וּבְכָל שָׁעָה:

V'al hakol Adonai Eloheynu anakhnu modim lakh, um'varkhim otakh, yitbarakh shimkha b'fi kol khai tamid l'olam vaed, kakatuv. V'akhalta v'svata, uverakhta et Adonai Elohekha al haarets hatova asher n'tan lakh, barukh ata Adonai, al haarets v'al hamazon.

18 וְעַל הַכֹּל יְיָ אֱלֹהֵינוּ אֲנַחְנוּ מוֹדִים לָךְ, וּמְבָרְכִים
19 אוֹתָךְ, יִתְבָּרַךְ שִׁמְךָ בְּפִי כָּל חַי תָּמִיד לְעוֹלָם
20 וָעֶד. כַּכָּתוּב: וְאָכַלְתָּ וְשָׂבָעְתָּ, וּבֵרַכְתָּ אֶת יְיָ
21 אֱלֹהֶיךָ עַל הָאָרֶץ הַטֹּבָה אֲשֶׁר נָתַן לָךְ. בָּרוּךְ
22 אַתָּה יְיָ, עַל הָאָרֶץ וְעַל הַמָּזוֹן:

Rakhem (na) Adonai Eloheynu, al Yisrael amekha, v'al Y'rushalayim irekha, v'al

23 רַחֵם (נָא) יְיָ אֱלֹהֵינוּ, עַל יִשְׂרָאֵל עַמֶּךָ, וְעַל
24 יְרוּשָׁלַיִם עִירֶךָ, וְעַל צִיּוֹן מִשְׁכַּן כְּבוֹדֶךָ, וְעַל

1 **Praised are you**, Eternal our God, Ruler of the universe, Who sustains the whole universe in His goodness, with grace, lovingkindness, and mercy. He gives food to all, for His mercy endures forever. In His great goodness He never failed us with sustenance and may He never fail us, forever and ever, for the sake of His great Name. It is He Who provides for all, sustains all, and is beneficent to all, preparing food for all His creatures whom He created. Praised art Thou, Eternal, Who provides food for all.

10 **We thank You**, Eternal our God, for the good land which You gave to our forefathers; and for bringing us out from the land of Egypt, O Eternal our God, and redeeming us from the house of bondage; and for your covenant sealed in our flesh; and for your Torah which You taught us; and for Your laws which You made known to us; and for the life of grace and lovingkindness which You have graciously bestowed upon us; and for the food we eat with which You nourish and sustain us at all times, daily, and at every season and at every hour.

18 **For all these blessings**, Eternal our God, we thank You and praise You. May Your Name be blessed by all the living at all times and for all time! Thus do we fulfill your command: "You shall eat and be satisfied, and bless the Eternal your God for the good land which He has given you." Praised are You, Eternal, for the land and for our sustenance.

23 **Eternal our God,** have mercy on Israel Your people, on Jerusalem Your city and Zion the dwelling place of Your

tsiyon mishkan k'vodekha, v'al malkhut beyt David m'shikhekha, v'al habayit hagadol v'hakadosh shenikra shimkha alav, Eloheynu, Avinu, r'enu, zunenu, parn'senu, v'khalklenu, v'harvikhenu, v'harvakh lanu Adonai Eloheynu m'hera mikol tsaroteynu, v'na al tatsrikhenu Adonai Eloheynu, lo lidey matnat basar vadam, v'lo lidey halvaatam, ki im l'yadkha ham'lea, hap'tukha, hak'dosha v'har'khava, shelo nevosh v'lo nikalem l'olam vaed.	1 מַלְכוּת בֵּית דָּוִד מְשִׁיחֶךָ, וְעַל הַבַּיִת הַגָּדוֹל 2 וְהַקָּדוֹשׁ שֶׁנִּקְרָא שִׁמְךָ עָלָיו. אֱלֹהֵינוּ, אָבִינוּ, 3 רְעֵנוּ, זוּנֵנוּ, פַּרְנְסֵנוּ, וְכַלְכְּלֵנוּ, וְהַרְוִיחֵנוּ, וְהַרְוַח 4 לָנוּ יְיָ אֱלֹהֵינוּ מְהֵרָה מִכָּל צָרוֹתֵינוּ. וְנָא אַל 5 תַּצְרִיכֵנוּ יְיָ אֱלֹהֵינוּ, לֹא לִידֵי מַתְּנַת בָּשָׂר וָדָם, 6 וְלֹא לִידֵי הַלְוָאָתָם. כִּי אִם לְיָדְךָ הַמְּלֵאָה, 7 הַפְּתוּחָה, הַקְּדוֹשָׁה וְהָרְחָבָה, שֶׁלֹּא נֵבוֹשׁ וְלֹא 8 נִכָּלֵם לְעוֹלָם וָעֶד:

The following paragraph is said on the Sabbath:

R'tsey v'hakhalitsenu Adonai Eloheynu b'mitsvtekha, uvmitsvat yom hash'vii haShabat hagadol v'hakadosh hazeh, ki yom ze gadol v'kadosh hu l'fanekha, lishbat bo v'lanuakh bo b'ahava k'mitsvat r'tsonekha, uvirtsonkha haniakh lanu Adonai Eloheynu, shelo t'hey tsara v'yagon vaanakha b'yom m'nukhatenu, v'harenu Adonai Eloheynu b'nekhamat tsiyon irekha, uv'vinyan Y'rushalayim ir kadshekha, ki ata hu baal hay'shuot uvaal hanekhamot.	9 רְצֵה וְהַחֲלִיצֵנוּ יְיָ אֱלֹהֵינוּ בְּמִצְוֹתֶיךָ, וּבְמִצְוַת 10 יוֹם הַשְּׁבִיעִי הַשַּׁבָּת הַגָּדוֹל וְהַקָּדוֹשׁ הַזֶּה. כִּי 11 יוֹם זֶה גָּדוֹל וְקָדוֹשׁ הוּא לְפָנֶיךָ, לִשְׁבָּת־בּוֹ 12 וְלָנוּחַ בּוֹ בְּאַהֲבָה כְּמִצְוַת רְצוֹנֶךָ. וּבִרְצוֹנְךָ 13 הָנִיחַ לָנוּ יְיָ אֱלֹהֵינוּ, שֶׁלֹּא תְהֵא צָרָה וְיָגוֹן 14 וַאֲנָחָה בְּיוֹם מְנוּחָתֵנוּ. וְהַרְאֵנוּ יְיָ אֱלֹהֵינוּ 15 בְּנֶחָמַת צִיּוֹן עִירֶךָ, וּבְבִנְיַן יְרוּשָׁלַיִם עִיר 16 קָדְשֶׁךָ, כִּי אַתָּה הוּא בַּעַל הַיְשׁוּעוֹת וּבַעַל 17 הַנֶּחָמוֹת:

Eloheynu vEylohey avoteynu, yaale v'yavo v'yagia, v'yerae, v'yeratse, v'yishama, v'yipaked, v'yizakher zikhronenu ufikdonenu, v'zikhron avoteynu, v'zikhron Mashiakh ben David avdekha, v'zikhron Y'rushalayim ir kadshekha, v'zikhron kol amkha beyt Yisrael l'fanekha, lifleta l'tova l'khen ulkhesed ulrakhamim, l'khayim ulshalom b'yom khag hamatsot hazeh, zakhrenu Adonai Eloheynu bo l'tova,	18 אֱלֹהֵינוּ וֵאלֹהֵי אֲבוֹתֵינוּ, יַעֲלֶה וְיָבֹא וְיַגִּיעַ, 19 וְיֵרָאֶה, וְיֵרָצֶה, וְיִשָּׁמַע, וְיִפָּקֵד, וְיִזָּכֵר זִכְרוֹנֵנוּ 20 וּפִקְדוֹנֵנוּ, וְזִכְרוֹן אֲבוֹתֵינוּ, וְזִכְרוֹן מָשִׁיחַ 21 בֶּן דָּוִד עַבְדֶּךָ, וְזִכְרוֹן יְרוּשָׁלַיִם עִיר קָדְשֶׁךָ, 22 וְזִכְרוֹן כָּל עַמְּךָ בֵּית יִשְׂרָאֵל לְפָנֶיךָ, לִפְלֵיטָה 23 לְטוֹבָה לְחֵן וּלְחֶסֶד וּלְרַחֲמִים, לְחַיִּים וּלְשָׁלוֹם 24 בְּיוֹם חַג הַמַּצּוֹת הַזֶּה. זָכְרֵנוּ יְיָ אֱלֹהֵינוּ בּוֹ 25 לְטוֹבָה, וּפָקְדֵנוּ בּוֹ לִבְרָכָה, וְהוֹשִׁיעֵנוּ בּוֹ

Continue on page 56

glory, on the royal house of David Your anointed, and on the great and holy Temple called by Your Name. Our God, our Father, be our Shepherd. Sustain us, support us, and provide for all our needs, and Eternal our God, give us speedy relief from all our troubles. Eternal our God, may we never be brought to depend on gifts or loans from the hand of flesh and blood, but only on Your hand, full, open, abundant, and generous. Thus shall we never be put to shame.

The following paragraph is said on the Sabbath:

9 **Eternal our God**, by Your grace, strengthen us in Your commandments, particularly in the observance of the seventh day, this great and holy Sabbath. For it is a great and holy day given by You in love for rest and serenity. May it be Your will, Eternal our God, to grant us such repose that there shall be no sorrow, trouble, or sighing on our day of rest. And, Eternal our God, may we see Zion Your city comforted, Jerusalem Your holy city rebuilt, for You are the God of salvation and consolation.

18 **Our God** and God of our ancestors, on this day of the Festival of Matzot may there come before You the remembrance of us and our ancestors, of Jerusalem Your holy city, of the Messiah son of David Your servant, and of all Your people of the house of Israel. May these come before You, and in tenderness, grace, and mercy be heard and accepted with favor by You for life and peace, for deliverance and happiness. Eternal our God, remember us this day for happiness, for blessing and the good life. With a word of salvation and mercy have pity on us and save us. Our eyes are lifted toward You, for You are a gracious and merciful God and Ruler.

ufakdenu vo livrakha, v'hoshienu vo l'khayim (tovim), uvidvar y'shua v'rakhamim, khus v'khanenu, v'rakhem aleynu v'hoshienu, ki elekha eyneynu, ki El Melekh khanun v'rakhum ata.	1 לְחַיִּים (טוֹבִים). וּבִדְבַר יְשׁוּעָה וְרַחֲמִים, חוּס 2 וְחָנֵּנוּ, וְרַחֵם עָלֵינוּ וְהוֹשִׁיעֵנוּ, כִּי אֵלֶיךָ עֵינֵינוּ, 3 כִּי אֵל מֶלֶךְ חַנּוּן וְרַחוּם אָתָּה:
Uv'ney Y'rushalayim ir hakodesh bimhera b'yameynu, barukh ata Adonai, boney b'rakhamav Y'rushalayim, amen.	4 **וּבְנֵה** יְרוּשָׁלַיִם עִיר הַקֹּדֶשׁ בִּמְהֵרָה בְּיָמֵינוּ. 5 בָּרוּךְ אַתָּה יְיָ, בּוֹנֵה בְרַחֲמָיו יְרוּשָׁלָיִם. אָמֵן.
Barukh ata Adonai, Eloheynu Melekh Haolam, haEl Avinu, malkenu, adirenu, borenu, goalenu, yotsrenu, k'doshenu, k'dosh Yaakov, roenu roey Yisrael, haMelekh hatov, v'hametiv lakol, she b'khol yom vayom hu hetiv, hu metiv, hu yeytiv lanu, hu gmalanu, hu gomlenu, hu yigm'lenu laad, l'khen ul-khesed ulrakhamim ulrevakh, hatsala v'hatslakha, brakha viyshua, nekhama, parnasa v'khalkala, v'rakhamim v'khay-im v'shalom v'khol tov, umikol tuv l'olam al y'khasrenu.	6 **בָּרוּךְ** אַתָּה יְיָ, אֱלֹהֵינוּ מֶלֶךְ הָעוֹלָם, הָאֵל 7 אָבִינוּ, מַלְכֵּנוּ, אַדִּירֵנוּ, בּוֹרְאֵנוּ, גּוֹאֲלֵנוּ, יוֹצְרֵנוּ, 8 קְדוֹשֵׁנוּ, קְדוֹשׁ יַעֲקֹב, רוֹעֵנוּ רוֹעֵה יִשְׂרָאֵל. 9 הַמֶּלֶךְ הַטּוֹב, וְהַמֵּטִיב לַכֹּל, שֶׁבְּכָל יוֹם וָיוֹם הוּא 10 הֵטִיב, הוּא מֵטִיב, הוּא יֵיטִיב לָנוּ. הוּא גְמָלָנוּ, 11 הוּא גוֹמְלֵנוּ, הוּא יִגְמְלֵנוּ לָעַד, לְחֵן וּלְחֶסֶד 12 וּלְרַחֲמִים וּלְרֶוַח, הַצָּלָה וְהַצְלָחָה, בְּרָכָה 13 וִישׁוּעָה, נֶחָמָה, פַּרְנָסָה וְכַלְכָּלָה, וְרַחֲמִים 14 וְחַיִּים וְשָׁלוֹם וְכָל טוֹב, וּמִכָּל טוּב לְעוֹלָם אַל 15 יְחַסְּרֵנוּ:
Harakhaman, hu yimlokh aleynu l'olam vaed, harakhaman, hu yitbarakh bashamayim uvaarets, harakhaman, hu yishtabakh l'dor dorim, v'yitpaar banu laad ulnetsakh n'tsakhim, v'yithadar banu laad ulolmey olamim, harakhaman, hu y'farn'senu b'khavod, harakhaman, hu yishbor ulenu meal tsavarenu v'hu yolikhenu (m'hera) kom'miyut l'artsenu, harakhaman, hu yishlakh lanu brakha m'ruba babayit hazeh, v'al shulkhan ze sheakhalnu alav, harakhaman, hu	16 **הָרַחֲמָן**, הוּא יִמְלוֹךְ עָלֵינוּ לְעוֹלָם וָעֶד. הָרַחֲמָן, 17 הוּא יִתְבָּרַךְ בַּשָּׁמַיִם וּבָאָרֶץ. הָרַחֲמָן, הוּא 18 יִשְׁתַּבַּח לְדוֹר דּוֹרִים, וְיִתְפָּאַר בָּנוּ לָעַד וּלְנֶצַח 19 נְצָחִים, וְיִתְהַדַּר בָּנוּ לָעַד וּלְעוֹלְמֵי עוֹלָמִים. 20 הָרַחֲמָן, הוּא יְפַרְנְסֵנוּ בְּכָבוֹד. הָרַחֲמָן, הוּא 21 יִשְׁבּוֹר עָלֵינוּ מֵעַל צַוָּארֵנוּ וְהוּא יוֹלִיכֵנוּ (מְהֵרָה) 22 קוֹמְמִיּוּת לְאַרְצֵנוּ. הָרַחֲמָן, הוּא יִשְׁלַח לָנוּ 23 בְּרָכָה מְרֻבָּה בַּבַּיִת הַזֶּה, וְעַל שֻׁלְחָן זֶה שֶׁאָכַלְנוּ 24 עָלָיו. הָרַחֲמָן, הוּא יִשְׁלַח לָנוּ אֶת אֵלִיָּהוּ הַנָּבִיא

Continue on page 58

4 **O rebuild** Jerusalem the holy city soon in our days! Praised are You, Eternal, Who will rebuild Jerusalem in His mercy. Amen.

6 **Praised are You**, Eternal our God, Ruler of the universe, God our Father, our Ruler, our Mighty One, our Creator, our Redeemer, our Maker, our Holy One, the Holy One of Jacob, our Shepherd and Shepherd of Israel, the good Ruler Who does good to all. Even as He has daily done good to us, so may He continue to do good to us forever. Even as He has dealt bountifully with us, so may He ever bestow on us with boundless grace, lovingkindness and mercy, help, prosperity, blessing, salvation, consolation, sustenance, and support, in life and peace and all that is good. And may we never know lack of anything good.

16 **May** the All-merciful rule over us forever. May the All-merciful be blessed in the heavens and on the earth. May the All-merciful be praised for all generations and glorified and honored among us for all eternity. May the All-merciful grant that our needs be supplied with dignity. May the All-merciful break the oppressor's yoke from our neck and lead us proudly to our land. May the All-merciful send the fullness of blessing on this household and bless this table at which we have eaten. May the All-merciful send to us the prophet Elijah, of blessed memory, bearing good tidings of deliverance and comfort.

<table>
<tr>
<td>

yishlakh lanu et Eliyahu Hanavi zakhur latov, vi'vaser lanu b'sorot tovot y'shuot v'nekhamot.

</td>
<td>

1 זְכוּר לַטוֹב, וִיבַשֶׂר־לָנוּ בְּשׂוֹרוֹת טוֹבוֹת
2 יְשׁוּעוֹת וְנֶחָמוֹת.

</td>
</tr>
<tr>
<td>

3 Harakhaman, hu y'varekh [oti, et avi mori, imi morati, ishti, baali, tseetsaai, baal habayit hazeh uvaalat habayit hazeh, kol ham'subin kan, otam v'et beytam v'et zaram v'et kol asher lahem, otanu v'et kol asher lanu, kmo shenitbarkhu avoteynu, Avraham Yitskhak v'Yaakov bakol, mikol, kol, ken y'varekh otanu kulanu yakhad bivrakha shlema, v'nomar amen.

</td>
<td>

3 **הָרַחֲמָן**, הוּא יְבָרֵךְ [אוֹתִי, אֶת אָבִי מוֹרִי,
4 אִמִּי מוֹרָתִי, אִשְׁתִּי, בַּעֲלִי, צֶאֱצָאַי, בַּעַל
5 הַבַּיִת הַזֶּה וּבַעֲלַת הַבַּיִת הַזֶּה, כָּל הַמְסֻבִּין
6 כָּאן, אוֹתָם וְאֶת בֵּיתָם וְאֶת זַרְעָם וְאֶת כָּל
7 אֲשֶׁר לָהֶם. אוֹתָנוּ וְאֶת כָּל אֲשֶׁר לָנוּ, כְּמוֹ
8 שֶׁנִּתְבָּרְכוּ אֲבוֹתֵינוּ, אַבְרָהָם יִצְחָק וְיַעֲקֹב
9 בַּכֹּל, מִכֹּל, כֹּל, כֵּן יְבָרֵךְ אוֹתָנוּ כֻּלָּנוּ יַחַד
10 בִּבְרָכָה שְׁלֵמָה, וְנֹאמַר אָמֵן:

</td>
</tr>
<tr>
<td>

Bamarom y'lamdu aleyhem v'aleynu zkhut, shethey l'mishmeret shalom, v'nisa vrakha meet Adonai uts'daka meElohey yishenu, v'nimtsa khen v'se-khel tov b'eyney Elohim vaadom.

</td>
<td>

11 **בַּמָּרוֹם** יְלַמְּדוּ עֲלֵיהֶם וְעָלֵינוּ זְכוּת, שֶׁתְּהֵא
12 לְמִשְׁמֶרֶת שָׁלוֹם, וְנִשָּׂא בְרָכָה מֵאֵת יְיָ
13 וּצְדָקָה מֵאֱלֹהֵי יִשְׁעֵנוּ, וְנִמְצָא חֵן וְשֵׂכֶל טוֹב
14 בְּעֵינֵי אֱלֹהִים וְאָדָם:

</td>
</tr>
<tr>
<td>

(on Shabat: Harakhaman, hu yankhilenu yom shekulo Shabat um'nukha l'khayey Haolamim.)

</td>
<td>

15 (בשבת: הָרַחֲמָן, הוּא יַנְחִילֵנוּ יוֹם שֶׁכֻּלּוֹ שַׁבָּת
16 וּמְנוּחָה לְחַיֵּי הָעוֹלָמִים.)

</td>
</tr>
<tr>
<td>

Harakhaman, hu yankhilenu yom she-kulo tov. Harakhaman, hu y'zakenu liy'mot haMashiakh ulkhayey Haolam haba. Migdol y'shuot malko, v'ose khesed lim'shikho, l'David ulzaro ad olam. Ose shalom bim'romav, hu yaase shalom, aleynu v'al kol Yisrael, v'imru amen.

</td>
<td>

17 **הָרַחֲמָן**, הוּא יַנְחִילֵנוּ יוֹם שֶׁכֻּלּוֹ טוֹב. הָרַחֲמָן,
18 הוּא יְזַכֵּנוּ לִימוֹת הַמָּשִׁיחַ וּלְחַיֵּי הָעוֹלָם
19 הַבָּא. מִגְדּוֹל יְשׁוּעוֹת מַלְכּוֹ, וְעֹשֶׂה חֶסֶד
20 לִמְשִׁיחוֹ, לְדָוִד וּלְזַרְעוֹ עַד עוֹלָם: עֹשֶׂה
21 שָׁלוֹם בִּמְרוֹמָיו, הוּא יַעֲשֶׂה שָׁלוֹם, עָלֵינוּ
22 וְעַל כָּל יִשְׂרָאֵל, וְאִמְרוּ אָמֵן:

</td>
</tr>
</table>

3 **May the All-merciful** bless this house and all assembled here, us and all that is ours. May He bless us all together with perfect blessing, even as our ancestors Abraham, Isaac, and Jacob were blessed with every manner of blessing, and let us say, Amen.

11 **On high** may there be invoked for them and for us such grace as shall ever be a safeguard of peace. Then shall we receive blessing from the Eternal and righteousness from the God of our salvation, and may we find grace and understanding in the eyes of God and of man.

(*On Shabbat:*) May the All-merciful grant us a day that shall be filled with Sabbath peace and and repose in eternal life.

15 **May** the All-merciful grant us a day that shall be only good. May the Creator of harmony in the heavens create peace for us and for all Israel, and let us say.

17 **May** the All-merciful make us worthy of seeing the days of the Messiah and life in the world to come. He is a tower of salvation to His king and shows kindness to His anointed, to David and his seed forever. May the Creator of harmony in the heavens create peace for us and for all Israel, and let us say, Amen.

1 **Yiru** et Adonai k'doshav, ki eyn makhsor liy'reav. K'firim rashu v'raevu, v'dorshey Adonai lo yakhsru khol tov. Hodu lAdonai ki tov, ki l'olam khasdo. Poteyakh et yadekha, umasbia l'khol khai ratson. Barukh hagever asher yivtakh bAdonai, v'haya Adonai mivtakho. Naar hayiti gam zakanti v'lo raiti tsadik neezav, v'zaro m'vakesh lakhem. Adonai oz l'amo yiten, Adonai y'varekh et amo vashalom.

1 יִרְאוּ אֶת יְיָ קְדֹשָׁיו, כִּי אֵין מַחְסוֹר לִירֵאָיו:
2 כְּפִירִים רָשׁוּ וְרָעֵבוּ, וְדוֹרְשֵׁי יְיָ לֹא יַחְסְרוּ
3 כָל טוֹב: הוֹדוּ לַיְיָ כִּי טוֹב, כִּי לְעוֹלָם חַסְדּוֹ:
4 פּוֹתֵחַ אֶת יָדֶךָ, וּמַשְׂבִּיעַ לְכָל חַי רָצוֹן: בָּרוּךְ
5 הַגֶּבֶר אֲשֶׁר יִבְטַח בַּיְיָ, וְהָיָה יְיָ מִבְטַחוֹ: נַעַר
6 הָיִיתִי גַם זָקַנְתִּי וְלֹא רָאִיתִי צַדִּיק נֶעֱזָב, וְזַרְעוֹ
7 מְבַקֶּשׁ לָחֶם: יְיָ עֹז לְעַמּוֹ יִתֵּן, יְיָ יְבָרֵךְ אֶת עַמּוֹ
8 בַשָּׁלוֹם:

THE THIRD CUP

Barukh ata Adonai, Eloheynu Melekh Haolam, borey pri hagafen.

9 בָּרוּךְ אַתָּה יְיָ, אֱלֹהֵינוּ מֶלֶךְ הָעוֹלָם, בּוֹרֵא פְּרִי
10 הַגָּפֶן:

Drink the wine while reclining on the left.

Pour the fourth cup and also Elijah's cup. The door is opened, all rise and the following is said:

Shfokh khamatkha el hagoyim asher lo y'daukha, v'al mamlakhot asher b'shimkha lo karau. Ki akhal et Yaakov, v'et navehu heshamu. Shfakh aleyhem zamekha, vakharon apkha yasigem. Tirdof b'af v'tashmidem, mitakhat shmey Adonai.

11 שְׁפֹךְ חֲמָתְךָ אֶל־הַגּוֹיִם אֲשֶׁר לֹא יְדָעוּךָ, וְעַל־
12 מַמְלָכוֹת אֲשֶׁר בְּשִׁמְךָ לֹא קָרָאוּ: כִּי אָכַל אֶת־
13 יַעֲקֹב, וְאֶת־נָוֵהוּ הֵשַׁמּוּ: שְׁפָךְ־עֲלֵיהֶם זַעְמֶךָ,
14 וַחֲרוֹן אַפְּךָ יַשִּׂיגֵם: תִּרְדֹּף בְּאַף וְתַשְׁמִידֵם,
15 מִתַּחַת שְׁמֵי יְיָ:

Close the door. All are seated.

1 **Revere** the Eternal, you His holy ones, for those who revere Him suffer no want. Even young lions may lack and know hunger, but they who seek the Eternal shall not lack any good. Give thanks to the Eternal for He is good, for His mercy endures forever. He opens His hand and satisfies every living thing. Blessed is the person who trusts in the Eternal, and the Eternal is his stronghold. I have been young, now I am old; and I have not seen a righteous man forsaken or his children begging for bread. The Eternal will give strength to His people; the Eternal will bless His people with peace.

THE THIRD CUP

9 **Praised are You,** Eternal our God, Ruler of the universe, Creator of the fruit of the vine.

Drink the wine while reclining on the left.

**Pour the fourth cup and also Elijah's cup. The door
is opened, all rise and the following is said:**

11 **Pour out Your anger** upon the nations that do not know Thee, and upon the nations that call not upon Your Name; for they have consumed Jacob and laid waste his habitation. Pour out Your anger upon them and let Your fury overtake them. Pursue them in anger and destroy them from under the heavens of the Eternal.

Close the door. All are seated.

הַלֵּל

HALLEL

1 לֹא לָנוּ יְיָ, לֹא לָנוּ כִּי לְשִׁמְךָ תֵּן כָּבוֹד, עַל

2 חַסְדְּךָ עַל אֲמִתֶּךָ: לָמָּה יֹאמְרוּ הַגּוֹיִם, אַיֵּה

3 נָא אֱלֹהֵיהֶם: וֵאלֹהֵינוּ בַשָּׁמָיִם, כֹּל אֲשֶׁר חָפֵץ

4 עָשָׂה: עֲצַבֵּיהֶם כֶּסֶף וְזָהָב, מַעֲשֵׂה יְדֵי אָדָם:

5 פֶּה לָהֶם וְלֹא יְדַבֵּרוּ, עֵינַיִם לָהֶם וְלֹא יִרְאוּ:

6 אָזְנַיִם לָהֶם וְלֹא יִשְׁמָעוּ, אַף לָהֶם וְלֹא יְרִיחוּן:

7 יְדֵיהֶם וְלֹא יְמִישׁוּן, רַגְלֵיהֶם וְלֹא יְהַלֵּכוּ, לֹא

8 יֶהְגּוּ בִּגְרוֹנָם: כְּמוֹהֶם יִהְיוּ עֹשֵׂיהֶם, כֹּל אֲשֶׁר

9 בֹּטֵחַ בָּהֶם: יִשְׂרָאֵל בְּטַח בַּיְיָ, עֶזְרָם וּמָגִנָּם

10 הוּא: בֵּית אַהֲרֹן בִּטְחוּ בַיְיָ, עֶזְרָם וּמָגִנָּם הוּא:

11 יִרְאֵי יְיָ בִּטְחוּ בַיְיָ, עֶזְרָם וּמָגִנָּם הוּא:

Lo lanu Adonai, lo lanu ki l'shimkha ten kavod, al khasd'kha al amitekha. Lama yomru hagoyim, ayey na Eloheyhem. VEyloheynu vashamayim, kol asher khafets asa. Atsabeyhem kesef v'zahav, maaseyy'dey adam. Pe lahem v'lo y'daberu, eynayim lahem v'lo yiru. Aznayim lahem v'lo yishmau, af lahem v'lo y'rikhun. Y'deyhem v'lo y'mishun, ragleyhem v'lo y'halekhu, lo yegu bigronam. Kmohem yihyu oseyhem, kol asher boteyakh bahem. Yisrael b'takh bAdonai, ezram umaginam hu. Beyt Aharon bitkhu vAdonai, ezram umaginam hu. Yirey Adonai bitkhu b'Adonai, ezram umaginam hu.

12 יְיָ זְכָרָנוּ יְבָרֵךְ, יְבָרֵךְ אֶת בֵּית יִשְׂרָאֵל, יְבָרֵךְ

13 אֶת בֵּית אַהֲרֹן: יְבָרֵךְ יִרְאֵי יְיָ, הַקְּטַנִּים עִם

14 הַגְּדֹלִים: יֹסֵף יְיָ עֲלֵיכֶם, עֲלֵיכֶם וְעַל בְּנֵיכֶם:

15 בְּרוּכִים אַתֶּם לַיְיָ, עֹשֵׂה שָׁמַיִם וָאָרֶץ: הַשָּׁמַיִם

16 שָׁמַיִם לַיְיָ, וְהָאָרֶץ נָתַן לִבְנֵי אָדָם: לֹא הַמֵּתִים

17 יְהַלְלוּ יָהּ, וְלֹא כָּל יֹרְדֵי דוּמָה: וַאֲנַחְנוּ נְבָרֵךְ יָהּ,

18 מֵעַתָּה וְעַד עוֹלָם, הַלְלוּיָהּ:

Adonai zkharanu y'varekh, y'varekh et beyt Yisrael, y'varekh et beyt Aharon. Y'varekh yirey Adonai, hak'tanim im hag'dolim. Yosef Adonai aleykhem, aleykhem v'al b'neykhem. Brukhim atem l'Adonai, osey shamayim vaarets. Hashamayim shamayim lAdonai, v'haarets natan livney adam. Lo hametim y'hal'lu ya, v'lo kol yordey duma. Vaanakhnu n'varekh ya, meata v'ad olam, hal'luya.

19 אָהַבְתִּי כִּי יִשְׁמַע יְיָ, אֶת קוֹלִי תַּחֲנוּנָי: כִּי

20 הִטָּה אָזְנוֹ לִי, וּבְיָמַי אֶקְרָא: אֲפָפוּנִי חֶבְלֵי

21 מָוֶת, וּמְצָרֵי שְׁאוֹל מְצָאוּנִי, צָרָה וְיָגוֹן אֶמְצָא:

22 וּבְשֵׁם יְיָ אֶקְרָא, אָנָּה יְיָ מַלְּטָה נַפְשִׁי: חַנּוּן

Ahavti ki yishma Adonai, et koli takhanunai. Ki hita ozno li, uvyamai ekra. Afafuni khevley mavet, um'tsarey sh'ol m'tsauni, tsara v'yagon emtsa. Uv'shem Adonai ekra, ana Adonai malta nafshi.

HALLEL

1 **Not for us**, O Eternal, not for us but for Yourself give glory, for Your mercy and Your truth. Why should the nations say, "Where, now, is their God?" Our God is in heaven and he does what He wills. Their idols are silver or gold, the work of human hands. They have a mouth but cannot speak; they have eyes but cannot see; they have ears but cannot hear; they have a nose but cannot smell; they have hands but cannot feel; they have feet but cannot walk; they cannot make a sound in their throat; like those who can make them and those who trust in them, let Israel trust in the Eternal; He is their help and shield.

12 **Let the house** of Aaron trust in the Eternal; He is their help and shield. Let those who revere the Eternal trust in the Eternal; He is their help and shield. The Eternal remembers us; He will bless the house of Israel and the house of Aaron. He will bless those who revere the Eternal, the lowly and the great. May the Eternal increase blessings upon you and your children. Blessed are you of the Eternal, the Maker of heaven and earth. The heavens are the heavens of the Eternal, and the earth He has given to the children of mortals. The dead cannot praise the Eternal, nor all who go down to silence. But we will praise the Eternal, now and forever. Halleluyah – Praise the Eternal.

19 **I love** the Eternal for He has heard my voice and my supplications. Because He has inclined His ear to me, I will call upon Him all my days. The struggles of death encompassed me, the agony of the grave seized me, trouble and sorrow met me. But I called upon the Name of the

1 Khanun Adonai v'tsadik, vEyloheynu m'rakhem. Shomer p'taim Adonai, daloti v'li y'hoshia. Shuvi nafshi limnukhaikhi, ki Adonai gamal alaikhi. Ki khilatsta nafshi mimavet, et eyni min dima, et ragli midekhi. Ethalekh lifney Adonai, b'artsot hakhayim. Heemanti ki adaber, ani aniti m'od. Ani amarti v'khofzi, kol haadam kozev.	יְיָ וְצַדִּיק, וֵאלֹהֵינוּ מְרַחֵם: שֹׁמֵר פְּתָאים יְיָ, דַּלּוֹתִי וְלִי יְהוֹשִׁיעַ: שׁוּבִי נַפְשִׁי לִמְנוּחָיְכִי, כִּי יְיָ גָּמַל עָלָיְכִי: כִּי חִלַּצְתָּ נַפְשִׁי מִמָּוֶת, אֶת עֵינִי מִן דִּמְעָה, אֶת רַגְלִי מִדֶּחִי: אֶתְהַלֵּךְ לִפְנֵי יְיָ, בְּאַרְצוֹת הַחַיִּים: הֶאֱמַנְתִּי כִּי אֲדַבֵּר, אֲנִי עָנִיתִי מְאֹד: אֲנִי אָמַרְתִּי בְחָפְזִי, כָּל הָאָדָם כֹּזֵב:	1 2 3 4 5 6
7 **Ma ashiv** l'Adonai, kol tagmulohi alai. Kos y'shuot esa, uv'shem Adonai ekra. N'darai l'Adonai ashalem, negda na l'khol amo. Yakar b'eyney Adonai, hamavta lakhasidav. Ana Adonai ki ani avdekha, ani avd'kha ben amatekha pitakhta l'moserai. L'kha ezbakh zevakh toda, uv'shem Adonai ekra. N'darai l'Adonai ashalem negda na l'khol amo. B'khatsrot beyt Adonai, b'tokhekhi Y'rushalayim, hal'luya.	**מָה אָשִׁיב** לַיְיָ, כָּל תַּגְמוּלוֹהִי עָלָי: כּוֹס יְשׁוּעוֹת אֶשָּׂא, וּבְשֵׁם יְיָ אֶקְרָא: נְדָרַי לַיְיָ אֲשַׁלֵּם, נֶגְדָה־ נָּא לְכָל עַמּוֹ: יָקָר בְּעֵינֵי יְיָ, הַמָּוְתָה לַחֲסִידָיו: אָנָּה יְיָ כִּי אֲנִי עַבְדֶּךָ, אֲנִי עַבְדְּךָ בֶּן אֲמָתֶךָ פִּתַּחְתָּ לְמוֹסֵרָי: לְךָ אֶזְבַּח זֶבַח תּוֹדָה, וּבְשֵׁם יְיָ אֶקְרָא: נְדָרַי לַיְיָ אֲשַׁלֵּם נֶגְדָה נָּא לְכָל עַמּוֹ: בְּחַצְרוֹת בֵּית יְיָ, בְּתוֹכֵכִי יְרוּשָׁלָיִם, הַלְלוּיָהּ:	7 8 9 10 11 12 13
Hal'lu et Adonai, kol goyim, shabkhuhu kol haumim. Ki gavar aleynu khasdo, veemet Adonai l'olam, hal'luya.	**הַלְלוּ** אֶת יְיָ, כָּל גּוֹים, שַׁבְּחוּהוּ כָּל הָאֻמִּים: כִּי גָבַר עָלֵינוּ חַסְדּוֹ, וֶאֱמֶת יְיָ לְעוֹלָם, הַלְלוּיָהּ:	14 15
Hodu lAdonai ki tov, ki l'olam khasdo. Yomar na Yisrael, ki l'olam khasdo. Yomru na veyt Aharon, ki l'olam khasdo. Yomru na yirey Adonai, ki l'olam khasdo.	**הוֹדוּ** לַיְיָ כִּי טוֹב, כִּי לְעוֹלָם חַסְדּוֹ: יֹאמַר נָא יִשְׂרָאֵל, כִּי לְעוֹלָם חַסְדּוֹ: יֹאמְרוּ נָא בֵית אַהֲרֹן, כִּי לְעוֹלָם חַסְדּוֹ: יֹאמְרוּ נָא יִרְאֵי יְיָ, כִּי לְעוֹלָם חַסְדּוֹ:	16 17 18 19
Min hametsar karati Ya, anani vamerkhav Ya. Adonai li lo ira, ma yaase li adam. Adonai li b'ozrai, vaani ere v'sonai. Tov lakhasot bAdonai, mibtoakh baadam. Tov lakhasot bAdonai, mibtoakh bin'divim.	**מִן הַמֵּצַר** קָרָאתִי יָּהּ, עָנָנִי בַמֶּרְחָב יָהּ: יְיָ לִי לֹא אִירָא, מַה יַּעֲשֶׂה לִי אָדָם: יְיָ לִי בְּעֹזְרָי, וַאֲנִי אֶרְאֶה בְשֹׂנְאָי: טוֹב לַחֲסוֹת בַּיְיָ, מִבְּטֹחַ בָּאָדָם: טוֹב לַחֲסוֹת בַּיְיָ, מִבְּטֹחַ בִּנְדִיבִים: כָּל גּוֹים	20 21 22 23

1 Eternal, "Eternal, I beg you, save me." Gracious is the Eternal and righteous; Our God is merciful. The Eternal watches over the simple; I was brought low and He saved me. O my soul, be at rest again for the Eternal has dealt kindly with You; for He has saved me from death, my eyes from tears and my foot from stumbling. I shall yet walk before the Eternal. In the lands of the living. I had faith even when I said, "I am greatly afflicted." Only in my haste did I say: "All humans are false."

7 **What can I render** unto the Eternal for all His goodness to me? I will lift up the cup of salvation and proclaim the Name of the Eternal. I will fulfill my vows unto the Eternal in the presence of all His people! Costly in the eyes of the Eternal is the death of His pious servants. I pray, O Eternal, for I am your servant. I, your servant, child of your handmaid; you have untied my bonds. To You I will offer thanksgiving sacrifice and call on the Name of the Eternal. I will fulfill my vows to the Eternal; In the presence of all His people, in the courts of the Eternal. In the midst of thee, O Jerusalem! Halleluyah – Praise the Eternal.

14 **Praise** the Eternal, all nations, Praise Him, all peoples, for great is His mercy toward us, and the faithfulness of the Eternal is forever. Halleluyah – Praise the Eternal.

16 **Give thanks** to the Eternal for He is good;
His mercy endures forever.

Let Israel say:
His mercy endures forever.

Let the house of Aaron say:
His mercy endures forever.

Let those who revere the Eternal say:
His mercy endures forever.

20 **Out of my straits** I called upon the Eternal; He answered me

1

#	Transliteration	Hebrew

Kol goyim svavuni, b'shem Adonai ki amilam. Sabuni gam svavuni, b'shem Adonai ki amilam. Sabuni khid'vorim doakhu k'esh kotsim, b'shem Adonai ki amilam. Dakho d'khitani linpol, vAdonai azarani. Ozi v'zimrat ya, vay'hi li liy'shua. Kol rina viyshua b'oholey tsadikim, y'min Adonai osa khayil. Y'min Adonai romema, y'min Adonai osa khayil. Lo amut ki ekhye, vaasaper maasey ya. Yasor yisrani ya, v'lamavet lo n'tanani. Pitkhu li shaarey tsedek, avo vam ode ya. Ze hashaar lAdonai, tsadikim yavou vo. Odkha ki anitani, vat'hi li liy'shua. Odkha ki anitani, vat'hi li liy'shua. Even maasu habonim, haita l'rosh pina. Even maasu habonim, haita l'rosh pina. Meet Adonai hayta zot, hi niflat b'eyneynu. Meet Adonai hayta zot, hi niflat b'eyneynu. Ze hayom asa Adonai, nagila v'nism'kha vo. Ze hayom asa Adonai, nagila v'nism'kha vo.

1 סְבָבוּנִי, בְּשֵׁם יְיָ כִּי אֲמִילַם: סַבּוּנִי גַם סְבָבוּנִי,
2 בְּשֵׁם יְיָ כִּי אֲמִילַם: סַבּוּנִי כִדְבֹרִים דֹּעֲכוּ כְּאֵשׁ
3 קוֹצִים, בְּשֵׁם יְיָ כִּי אֲמִילַם: דָּחֹה דְחִיתַנִי לִנְפֹּל,
4 וַיְיָ עֲזָרָנִי: עָזִּי וְזִמְרָת יָה, וַיְהִי לִי לִישׁוּעָה: קוֹל
5 רִנָּה וִישׁוּעָה בְּאָהֳלֵי צַדִּיקִים, יְמִין יְיָ עֹשָׂה חָיִל:
6 יְמִין יְיָ רוֹמֵמָה, יְמִין יְיָ עֹשָׂה חָיִל: לֹא אָמוּת כִּי
7 אֶחְיֶה, וַאֲסַפֵּר מַעֲשֵׂי יָה: יַסֹּר יִסְּרַנִּי יָּה, וְלַמָּוֶת
8 לֹא נְתָנָנִי: פִּתְחוּ לִי שַׁעֲרֵי צֶדֶק, אָבֹא בָם אוֹדֶה
9 יָּה: זֶה הַשַּׁעַר לַיְיָ, צַדִּיקִים יָבֹאוּ בוֹ: אוֹדְךָ כִּי
10 עֲנִיתָנִי, וַתְּהִי לִי לִישׁוּעָה: אוֹדְךָ כִּי עֲנִיתָנִי,
11 וַתְּהִי לִי לִישׁוּעָה: אֶבֶן מָאֲסוּ הַבּוֹנִים, הָיְתָה
12 לְרֹאשׁ פִּנָּה: אֶבֶן מָאֲסוּ הַבּוֹנִים, הָיְתָה לְרֹאשׁ
13 פִּנָּה: מֵאֵת יְיָ הָיְתָה זֹּאת, הִיא נִפְלָאת בְּעֵינֵינוּ:
14 מֵאֵת יְיָ הָיְתָה זֹּאת, הִיא נִפְלָאת בְּעֵינֵינוּ: זֶה
15 הַיּוֹם עָשָׂה יְיָ, נָגִילָה וְנִשְׂמְחָה בוֹ: זֶה הַיּוֹם
16 עָשָׂה יְיָ, נָגִילָה וְנִשְׂמְחָה בוֹ:

Ana Adonai hoshia na.
Ana Adonai hoshia na.
Ana Adonai hatslikha na.
Ana Adonai hatslikha na.

17 אָנָּא יְיָ הוֹשִׁיעָה נָּא:
18 אָנָּא יְיָ הוֹשִׁיעָה נָּא:
19 אָנָּא יְיָ הַצְלִיחָה נָּא:
20 אָנָּא יְיָ הַצְלִיחָה נָּא:

Barukh haba b'shem Adonai, berakhnukhem mibeyt Adonai. Barukh haba b'shem Adonai, berakhnukhem mibeyt Adonai. El Adonai vayaer lanu, isru khag baavotim, ad karnot hamizbeyakh. El Adonai vayaer lanu, isru khag baavotim,

21 בָּרוּךְ הַבָּא בְּשֵׁם יְיָ, בֵּרַכְנוּכֶם מִבֵּית יְיָ: בָּרוּךְ
22 הַבָּא בְּשֵׁם יְיָ, בֵּרַכְנוּכֶם מִבֵּית יְיָ: אֵל יְיָ וַיָּאֶר
23 לָנוּ, אִסְרוּ חַג בַּעֲבֹתִים, עַד קַרְנוֹת הַמִּזְבֵּחַ:
24 אֵל יְיָ וַיָּאֶר לָנוּ, אִסְרוּ חַג בַּעֲבֹתִים, עַד קַרְנוֹת
25 הַמִּזְבֵּחַ: אֵלִי אַתָּה וְאוֹדֶךָּ, אֱלֹהַי אֲרוֹמְמֶךָּ: אֵלִי

Continue on page 68

by setting me free. The Eternal is for me, I shall not fear. What can man do to me? The Eternal is my helper and I shall see victory over my enemies. It is better to trust in the Eternal than to rely on mortals. It is better to trust in the Eternal than to rely on princes. The nations beset me; in the Name of the Eternal I will surely cut them down. They surround me, yea, they encompass me; in the Name of the Eternal I will surely cut them down. They encompass me about like bees; they will be quenched as a fire of thorns; in the Name of the Eternal I will surely cut them down. They thrust at me that I might fall, but the Eternal supports me. The Eternal is my strength and song. He has become my salvation. Listen, the joyous song of victory is heard in the tents of the righteous; the right hand of the Eternal does valiantly. The right hand of the Eternal is exalted; the right hand of the Eternal does valiantly. I shall not die, but live and declare the works of the Eternal. Though the Eternal has indeed chastened me, He has not given me over to death. Open to me the gates of righteousness. I will enter them to praise the Eternal. This is the gate of the Eternal, the righteous shall enter it. I will give thanks to You for You have answered me and become my salvation. The stone which the builders rejected has become the cornerstone. This is the work of the Eternal; it is marvelous in our eyes. This is the day the Eternal has made; let us rejoice and be glad in it.

17 Eternal, we beg You, save us.

Eternal, we beg You, save us.

Eternal, we beg You, prosper us.

Eternal, we beg You, prosper us.

21 **Blessed** be you who come in the name of the Eternal; we bless you from the house of the Eternal. The Eternal is God and has given us light. Bring the sacrifice bound with myrtle

Continue on page 69

ad karnot hamizbeyakh. Eli ata v'odeka, Elohai arom'meka. Eli ata v'odeka, Elohai arom'meka. Hodu lAdonai ki tov, ki l'olam khasdo. Hodu lAdonai ki tov, ki l'olam khasdo.	1 אַתָּה וְאוֹדֶךָּ, אֱלֹהַי אֲרוֹמְמֶךָּ: הוֹדוּ לַיָי כִּי טוֹב, 2 כִּי לְעוֹלָם חַסְדּוֹ: הוֹדוּ לַיָי כִּי טוֹב, כִּי לְעוֹלָם 3 חַסְדּוֹ:
Y'hal'lukha Adonai Eloheynu (al) kol maasekha, vakhasidekha tsadikim osey r'tsonekha, v'khol amkha beyt Yisrael b'rina yodu vivarkhu vishabkhu vifaaru virom'mu v'yaaritsu v'yakdishu v'yamlikhu et shimkha malkenu, ki l'kha tov l'hodot ulshimkha nae l'zamer, ki meolam v'ad olam ata El.	4 יְהַלְלוּךְ יְיָ אֱלֹהֵינוּ (עַל) כָּל מַעֲשֶׂיךָ, וַחֲסִידֶיךָ 5 צַדִּיקִים עוֹשֵׂי רְצוֹנֶךָ, וְכָל עַמְּךָ בֵּית יִשְׂרָאֵל 6 בְּרִנָּה יוֹדוּ וִיבָרְכוּ וִישַׁבְּחוּ וִיפָאֲרוּ וִירוֹמְמוּ 7 וְיַעֲרִיצוּ וְיַקְדִּישׁוּ וְיַמְלִיכוּ אֶת שִׁמְךָ מַלְכֵּנוּ, כִּי 8 לְךָ טוֹב לְהוֹדוֹת וּלְשִׁמְךָ נָאֶה לְזַמֵּר, כִּי מֵעוֹלָם 9 וְעַד עוֹלָם אַתָּה אֵל.
Hodu lAdonai ki tov, ki l'olam khasdo.	10 הוֹדוּ לַיָי כִּי טוֹב, כִּי לְעוֹלָם חַסְדּוֹ:
Hodu lEylohey haElohim, ki l'olam khasdo.	11 הוֹדוּ לֵאלֹהֵי הָאֱלֹהִים, כִּי לְעוֹלָם חַסְדּוֹ:
Hodu laAdoney haadonim, ki l'olam khasdo.	12 הוֹדוּ לַאֲדֹנֵי הָאֲדֹנִים, כִּי לְעוֹלָם חַסְדּוֹ:
L'osey niflaot g'dolot l'vado, ki l'olam khasdo.	13 לְעֹשֵׂה נִפְלָאוֹת גְּדֹלוֹת לְבַדּוֹ, כִּי לְעוֹלָם חַסְדּוֹ:
L'osey hashamayim bitvuna, ki l'olam khasdo.	14 לְעֹשֵׂה הַשָּׁמַיִם בִּתְבוּנָה, כִּי לְעוֹלָם חַסְדּוֹ:
L'roka haarets al hamayim, ki l'olam khasdo.	15 לְרֹקַע הָאָרֶץ עַל הַמָּיִם, כִּי לְעוֹלָם חַסְדּוֹ:
L'osey orim g'dolim, ki l'olam khasdo.	16 לְעֹשֵׂה אוֹרִים גְּדֹלִים, כִּי לְעוֹלָם חַסְדּוֹ:
Et hashemesh l'memshelet bayom, ki l'olam khasdo.	17 אֶת הַשֶּׁמֶשׁ לְמֶמְשֶׁלֶת בַּיּוֹם, כִּי לְעוֹלָם חַסְדּוֹ:

to the very horns of the altar. You are my God and I will give thanks unto You; My God, I will praise You. Give thanks to the Eternal for He is good; His mercy endures forever.

4 **All Your works**, Eternal our God, shall praise You: Your pious servants, the righteous who do Your will, indeed all Your people, the House of Israel, with joyful thanks shall give thanks, bless, praise, glorify, extol, revere, sanctify and enthrone Your name, our Ruler, for unto You it is good to give thanks, and unto Your name it is proper to sing praises, for You are God from everlasting to everlasting. Blessed are You, Eternal our God, extolled in praises.

10 **Give thanks** to the Eternal for He is good;
   For His mercy endures forever.

11 Give thanks to the God of gods;
   For His mercy endures forever.

12 Give thanks to the Lord of lords;
   For His mercy endures forever.

13 To Him Who alone performs great miracles;
   For His mercy endures forever.

14 To Him Who made the heavens with wisdom;
   For His mercy endures forever.

15 To Him Who spread the earth above the waters;
   For His mercy endures forever.

16 To Him Who made the great lights;
   For His mercy endures forever.

17 The sun to rule by day;
   For His mercy endures forever.

Et hayareyakh v'khokhavim l'memshlot balayla, ki l'olam khasdo.	1	אֶת הַיָּרֵחַ וְכוֹכָבִים לְמֶמְשְׁלוֹת בַּלַּיְלָה, כִּי לְעוֹלָם חַסְדּוֹ:
L'makey Mitsrayim biv'khoreyhem, ki l'olam khasdo.	2	לְמַכֵּה מִצְרַיִם בִּבְכוֹרֵיהֶם, כִּי לְעוֹלָם חַסְדּוֹ:
Vayotsey Yisrael mitokham, ki l'olam khasdo.	3	וַיּוֹצֵא יִשְׂרָאֵל מִתּוֹכָם, כִּי לְעוֹלָם חַסְדּוֹ:
B'yad khazaka uvizroa n'tuya, ki l'olam khasdo.	4	בְּיָד חֲזָקָה וּבִזְרוֹעַ נְטוּיָה, כִּי לְעוֹלָם חַסְדּוֹ:
L'gozer yam suf ligzarim, ki l'olam khasdo.	5	לְגֹזֵר יַם סוּף לִגְזָרִים, כִּי לְעוֹלָם חַסְדּוֹ:
V'heevir Yisrael b'tokho, ki l'olam khasdo.	6	וְהֶעֱבִיר יִשְׂרָאֵל בְּתוֹכוֹ, כִּי לְעוֹלָם חַסְדּוֹ:
V'nier paro v'kheylo v'yam suf, ki l'olam khasdo.	7	וְנִעֵר פַּרְעֹה וְחֵילוֹ בְיַם סוּף, כִּי לְעוֹלָם חַסְדּוֹ:
L'molikh amo bamidbar, ki l'olam khasdo.	8	לְמוֹלִיךְ עַמּוֹ בַּמִּדְבָּר, כִּי לְעוֹלָם חַסְדּוֹ:
L'makey m'lakhim g'dolim, ki l'olam khasdo.	9	לְמַכֵּה מְלָכִים גְּדֹלִים, כִּי לְעוֹלָם חַסְדּוֹ:
Vayaharog m'lakhim adirim, ki l'olam khasdo.	10	וַיַּהֲרֹג מְלָכִים אַדִּירִים, כִּי לְעוֹלָם חַסְדּוֹ:
L'Sikhon Melekh haEmori, ki l'olam khasdo.	11	לְסִיחוֹן מֶלֶךְ הָאֱמֹרִי, כִּי לְעוֹלָם חַסְדּוֹ:
Ul'Og Melekh haBashan, ki l'olam khasdo.	12	וּלְעוֹג מֶלֶךְ הַבָּשָׁן, כִּי לְעוֹלָם חַסְדּוֹ:
V'natan artsam l'nakhala, ki l'olam khasdo.	13	וְנָתַן אַרְצָם לְנַחֲלָה, כִּי לְעוֹלָם חַסְדּוֹ:

1 The moon and stars to rule by night;
   For His mercy endures forever.

2 To Him Who smote Egypt through their firstborn;
   For His mercy endures forever.

3 And brought Israel forth from among them;
   For His mercy endures forever.

4 With a mighty hand and an outstretched arm;
   For His mercy endures forever.

5 To Him Who divided the Red Sea;
   For His mercy endures forever.

6 And brought Israel through it;
   For His mercy endures forever.

7 Who drowned Pharaoh and his host in the Red Sea;
   For His mercy endures forever.

8 To Him Who led His people through the wilderness;
   For His mercy endures forever.

9 To Him Who smote great kings;
   For His mercy endures forever.

10 And slew mighty kings;
   For His mercy endures forever.

11 Sihon, king of the Amorites;
   For His mercy endures forever.

12 And Og, king of Bashan;
   For His mercy endures forever.

13 And gave their land as a heritage;
   For His mercy endures forever.

1	נַחֲלָה לְיִשְׂרָאֵל עַבְדּוֹ, כִּי לְעוֹלָם חַסְדּוֹ:	Nakhala l'Yisrael avdo, ki l'olam khasdo.
2	שֶׁבְּשִׁפְלֵנוּ זָכַר לָנוּ, כִּי לְעוֹלָם חַסְדּוֹ:	Shebshiflenu zakhar lanu, ki l'olam khasdo.
3	וַיִּפְרְקֵנוּ מִצָּרֵינוּ, כִּי לְעוֹלָם חַסְדּוֹ:	Vayifr'kenu mitsareynu, ki l'olam khasdo.
4	נוֹתֵן לֶחֶם לְכָל בָּשָׂר, כִּי לְעוֹלָם חַסְדּוֹ:	Noten lekhem l'khol basar, ki l'olam khasdo.
5	הוֹדוּ לְאֵל הַשָּׁמָיִם, כִּי לְעוֹלָם חַסְדּוֹ:	Hodu l'El hashamayim, ki l'olam khasdo.

Nishmat kol khai t'varekh et shimkha Adonai Eloheynu, v'ruakh kol basar t'faer utromem zikhr'kha malkenu tamid, min Haolam v'ad Haolam ata El, umibaladekha eyn lanu Melekh goel umoshia, pode umatsil um'farnes um'rakhem, b'khol et tsara v'tsuka, eyn lanu Melekh ela ata. Elohey harishonim v'haakharonim, Eloha kol b'riyot, adon kol toladot, ham'hulal b'rov hatishbakhot, ham'naheg olamo b'khesed, uv'riyotav b'rakhamim, vAdonai lo yanum v'lo yishan, ham'orer y'shenim v'hamekits nirdamim v'hamesiakh ilmim, v'hamatir asurim, v'hasomekh noflim, v'hazokef k'fufim l'kha l'vadkha anakhnu modim.

6 **נִשְׁמַת** כָּל חַי תְּבָרֵךְ אֶת שִׁמְךָ יְיָ אֱלֹהֵינוּ, וְרוּחַ
7 כָּל בָּשָׂר תְּפָאֵר וּתְרוֹמֵם זִכְרְךָ מַלְכֵּנוּ תָּמִיד. מִן
8 הָעוֹלָם וְעַד הָעוֹלָם אַתָּה אֵל, וּמִבַּלְעָדֶיךָ אֵין
9 לָנוּ מֶלֶךְ גּוֹאֵל וּמוֹשִׁיעַ, פּוֹדֶה וּמַצִּיל וּמְפַרְנֵס
10 וּמְרַחֵם, בְּכָל עֵת צָרָה וְצוּקָה. אֵין לָנוּ מֶלֶךְ
11 אֶלָּא אָתָּה: אֱלֹהֵי הָרִאשׁוֹנִים וְהָאַחֲרוֹנִים,
12 אֱלוֹהַּ כָּל בְּרִיּוֹת, אֲדוֹן כָּל תּוֹלָדוֹת, הַמְהֻלָּל בְּרֹב
13 הַתִּשְׁבָּחוֹת, הַמְנַהֵג עוֹלָמוֹ בְּחֶסֶד, וּבְרִיּוֹתָיו
14 בְּרַחֲמִים. וַיְיָ לֹא יָנוּם וְלֹא יִישָׁן. הַמְעוֹרֵר
15 יְשֵׁנִים וְהַמֵּקִיץ נִרְדָּמִים וְהַמֵּשִׂיחַ אִלְּמִים,
16 וְהַמַּתִּיר אֲסוּרִים, וְהַסּוֹמֵךְ נוֹפְלִים, וְהַזּוֹקֵף
17 כְּפוּפִים לְךָ לְבַדְּךָ אֲנַחְנוּ מוֹדִים.

Ilu finu maley shira kayam, ulshonenu rina kahamon galav, v'siftoteynu shevakh k'merkhavey rakia, v'eyneynu m'irot kashemesh v'khayareyakh, v'yadeynu frusot k'nishrey shamayim, v'ragleynu kalot

18 **אִלּוּ פִינוּ** מָלֵא שִׁירָה כַּיָּם, וּלְשׁוֹנֵנוּ רִנָּה כַּהֲמוֹן
19 גַּלָּיו, וְשִׂפְתוֹתֵינוּ שֶׁבַח כְּמֶרְחֲבֵי רָקִיעַ, וְעֵינֵינוּ
20 מְאִירוֹת כַּשֶּׁמֶשׁ וְכַיָּרֵחַ, וְיָדֵינוּ פְרוּשׂוֹת כְּנִשְׁרֵי
21 שָׁמָיִם, וְרַגְלֵינוּ קַלּוֹת כָּאַיָּלוֹת, אֵין אֲנַחְנוּ

1 A heritage to Israel, His servant;
For His mercy endures forever.

2 Who remembered us in our lowliness;
For His mercy endures forever.

3 And redeemed us from those who oppressed us;
For His mercy endures forever.

4 Who gives food to all;
For His mercy endures forever.

5 Give thanks to the God of the heavens,
For His mercy endures forever.

6 **The soul** of all living things shall bless Your Name, Eternal our God; the spirit of all flesh shall ever adore and extol Your fame, our King. From everlasting to everlasting You are God, and besides You we have no Ruler or Deliverer, Redeemer, Sustainer, Who is merciful every time of sorrow and distress; we have no Ruler except You. O God of the beginning and of the end, God of all creatures, Master of all existence, Who is praised with numerous praises, Who leads the world with lovingkindness, and His creatures with mercy; God Who neither slumbers nor sleeps, awakens the sleeping and stirs the slumbering, gives speech to the dumb and loosens the bound, supports the falling and upholds the bowed-down, to You alone we give thanks.

18 **Were our mouths** filled with singing as the sea and our tongue uplifted in song as the waves and our lips with praise as the spacious firmament, and our eyes shining as the sun and the moon, and our hands stretched out as the eagles of the skies, and our feet swift as the hinds, we would

1	מַסְפִּיקִים, לְהוֹדוֹת לְךָ יְיָ אֱלֹהֵינוּ וֵאלֹהֵי
2	אֲבוֹתֵינוּ, וּלְבָרֵךְ אֶת שְׁמֶךָ עַל אַחַת מֵאֶלֶף אֶלֶף
3	אַלְפֵי אֲלָפִים וְרִבֵּי רְבָבוֹת פְּעָמִים הַטּוֹבוֹת,
4	שֶׁעָשִׂיתָ עִם אֲבוֹתֵינוּ וְעִמָּנוּ.
5	**מִמִּצְרַיִם** גְּאַלְתָּנוּ יְיָ אֱלֹהֵינוּ, וּמִבֵּית עֲבָדִים
6	פְּדִיתָנוּ, בְּרָעָב זַנְתָּנוּ, וּבְשָׂבָע כִּלְכַּלְתָּנוּ, מֵחֶרֶב
7	הִצַּלְתָּנוּ, וּמִדֶּבֶר מִלַּטְתָּנוּ, וּמֵחֳלָיִם רָעִים
8	וְנֶאֱמָנִים דִּלִּיתָנוּ. עַד הֵנָּה עֲזָרוּנוּ רַחֲמֶיךָ,
9	וְלֹא עֲזָבוּנוּ חֲסָדֶיךָ, וְאַל תִּטְּשֵׁנוּ יְיָ אֱלֹהֵינוּ
10	לָנֶצַח. עַל כֵּן אֵבָרִים שֶׁפִּלַּגְתָּ בָּנוּ, וְרוּחַ וּנְשָׁמָה
11	שֶׁנָּפַחְתָּ בְּאַפֵּינוּ, וְלָשׁוֹן אֲשֶׁר שַׂמְתָּ בְּפִינוּ,
12	הֵן הֵם יוֹדוּ וִיבָרְכוּ וִישַׁבְּחוּ וִיפָאֲרוּ וִירוֹמְמוּ
13	וְיַעֲרִיצוּ וְיַקְדִּישׁוּ וְיַמְלִיכוּ אֶת שִׁמְךָ מַלְכֵּנוּ.
14	כִּי כָל פֶּה לְךָ יוֹדֶה, וְכָל לָשׁוֹן לְךָ תִשָּׁבַע וְכָל
15	בֶּרֶךְ לְךָ תִכְרַע, וְכָל קוֹמָה לְפָנֶיךָ תִשְׁתַּחֲוֶה,
16	וְכָל לְבָבוֹת יִירָאוּךָ, וְכָל קֶרֶב וּכְלָיוֹת יְזַמְּרוּ
17	לִשְׁמֶךָ. כַּדָּבָר שֶׁכָּתוּב: כָּל עַצְמֹתַי תֹּאמַרְנָה
18	יְיָ מִי כָמוֹךָ. מַצִּיל עָנִי מֵחָזָק מִמֶּנּוּ, וְעָנִי וְאֶבְיוֹן
19	מִגֹּזְלוֹ: מִי יִדְמֶה לָּךְ, וּמִי יִשְׁוֶה לָּךְ, וּמִי יַעֲרָךְ
20	לָךְ: הָאֵל הַגָּדוֹל הַגִּבּוֹר וְהַנּוֹרָא, אֵל עֶלְיוֹן, קֹנֵה
21	שָׁמַיִם וָאָרֶץ: נְהַלֶּלְךָ וּנְשַׁבֵּחֲךָ וּנְפָאֶרְךָ וּנְבָרֵךְ
22	אֶת־שֵׁם קָדְשֶׁךָ. כָּאָמוּר: לְדָוִד, בָּרְכִי נַפְשִׁי אֶת
23	יְיָ, וְכָל קְרָבַי אֶת שֵׁם קָדְשׁוֹ:
24	**הָאֵל בְּתַעֲצֻמוֹת** עֻזֶּךָ, הַגָּדוֹל בִּכְבוֹד שְׁמֶךָ,
25	הַגִּבּוֹר לָנֶצַח וְהַנּוֹרָא בְּנוֹרְאוֹתֶיךָ, הַמֶּלֶךְ הַיּוֹשֵׁב
26	עַל כִּסֵּא רָם וְנִשָּׂא:

kaayalot, eyn anakhnu maspikim, l'hodot l'kha Adonai Eloheynu vEylohey avoteynu, ul'varekh et shmekha al akhat mealef elef alfey alafim v'ribey r'vavot p'amim hatovot, sheasita im avoteynu v'imanu.

5 **miMitsrayim** g'altanu Adonai Eloheynu, umibeyt avadim p'ditanu, b'raav zantanu, uvsava kilkaltanu, mekherev hitsaltanu, umidever milattanu, umekholayim raim v'neemanim dilitanu, ad hena azarunu rakhamekha, v'lo azavunu khasadekha, v'al titshenu Adonai Eloheynu lanetsakh, al ken evarim shepilagta banu, v'ruakh un'shama shenafakhta b'apeynu, v'lashon asher samta b'finu, hen hem yodu vivarkhu vishabkhu vifaaru virom'mu v'yaaritsu v'yakdishu v'yamlikhu et shimkha malkenu, ki khol pe l'kha yode, v'khol lashon l'kha tishava v'khol berekh l'kha tikhra, v'khol koma l'fanekha tishtakhave, v'khol l'vavot yiraukha, v'khol kerev ukhlayot y'zamru lishmekha, kadavar shekatuv. Kol atsmotai tomarna Adonai mi khamokha, matsil ani mekhazak mimenu, v'ani v'evyon migozlo. Mi yidme lakh, umi yishve lakh, umi yaarakh lakh. HaEl hagadol hagibor v'hanora, El elyon, koney shamayim vaarets. N'halelkha unshabekhakha un'faerkha un'varekh et shem kadshekha, kaamur. l'David, barkhi nafshi et Adonai, v'khol kravai et shem kodsho.

HaEl b'taatsumot uzekha, hagadol bikh'vod shmekha, hagibor lanetsakh v'hanora b'norotekha, haMelekh ha-yoshev al kisey ram v'nisa.

still not be able to offer proper thanks to You, Eternal our God and God of our ancestors and to praise Your Name one thousandth share or even a tenth of one thousandth share for the manifold goodness You bestowed upon our forefathers and upon us.

5 **From Egypt** You redeemed us, O Eternal our God, and from the house of bondage You liberated us. In famine You fed us, in plenty You sustained us, from the sword You saved us, from pestilence You delivered us, from severe sickness You spared us. Heretofore Your mercy helped us and Your lovingkindness did not forsake us. Do not forsake us evermore, we pray You, Eternal our God. Therefore, the limbs You have fashioned within us, and the spirit of life which You have breathed into us, and the tongue which You have placed in our mouth, they shall all thank, praise, extol, glorify, exalt, adore, hallow, and give sovereignty to Your Name, for every mouth shall give thanks to You, and every tongue shall pledge fealty to You; and every knee shall bend to You, and every living being shall bow down to You; all hearts shall revere You, and all innermost being shall sing to Your Name as it is written: "All my being shall say, Eternal, who is like You, delivering the afflicted from one stronger than he, and the needy from one who would rob him!" Who is like You, and who can equal You? Who can compare with You, O God, great, mighty, revered, supreme God, Master of heaven and earth? Let us praise and worship, glorify and bless Your holy Name, as it is said by David: "O my soul, bless the Eternal, and all that is within me, bless His holy name."

24 **You are God by the power** of Your might, great by the glory of Your Name, almighty forever and inspiring awe by Your deeds. You are the Ruler enthroned sublimely and exalted.

1 Shokhen ad, marom v'kadosh shmo, v'khatuv. Ran'nu tsadikim bAdonai, laysharim nava t'hila.

1 שׁוֹכֵן עַד, מָרוֹם וְקָדוֹשׁ שְׁמוֹ. וְכָתוּב: רַנְּנוּ
2 צַדִּיקִים בַּיְיָ, לַיְשָׁרִים נָאוָה תְהִלָּה.

3 B'fi y'sharim tithalal.
Uvdivrey tsadikim titbarakh.
Uvilshon khasidim titromam.
Uvkerev k'doshim titkadash.

3 בְּפִי יְשָׁרִים תִּתְהַלָּל.
4 וּבְדִבְרֵי צַדִּיקִים תִּתְבָּרַךְ.
5 וּבִלְשׁוֹן חֲסִידִים תִּתְרוֹמָם.
6 וּבְקֶרֶב קְדוֹשִׁים תִּתְקַדָּשׁ:

7 Uvmakhalot riv'vot amkha beyt Yisrael, b'rina yitpaar shimkha malkenu b'khol dor vador, sheken khovat kol hay'tsurim, l'fanekha Adonai Eloheynu, vEylohey avoteynu, l'hodot l'halel l'shabeyakh, l'faer l'romem l'hader, l'varekh l'aley ul'kales, al kol divrey shirot v'tishb'khot David ben Yishai, avd'kha m'shikhekha.

7 וּבְמַקְהֵלוֹת רִבְבוֹת עַמְּךָ בֵּית יִשְׂרָאֵל, בְּרִנָּה
8 יִתְפָּאַר שִׁמְךָ מַלְכֵּנוּ בְּכָל דּוֹר וָדוֹר. שֶׁכֵּן חוֹבַת
9 כָּל הַיְצוּרִים, לְפָנֶיךָ יְיָ אֱלֹהֵינוּ, וֵאלֹהֵי אֲבוֹתֵינוּ,
10 לְהוֹדוֹת לְהַלֵּל לְשַׁבֵּחַ, לְפָאֵר לְרוֹמֵם לְהַדֵּר,
11 לְבָרֵךְ לְעַלֵּה וּלְקַלֵּס, עַל כָּל דִּבְרֵי שִׁירוֹת
12 וְתִשְׁבְּחוֹת דָּוִד בֶּן יִשַׁי, עַבְדְּךָ מְשִׁיחֶךָ:

8 Yishtabakh shimkha laad malkenu, haEl haMelekh hagadol v'hakadosh bashamayim uvaarets, ki l'kha nae, Adonai Eloheynu vEylohey avoteynu, shir ushvakha, halel v'zimra, oz umemshala, netsakh, g'dula ugvura, t'hila v'tiferet, k'dusha umalkhut, b'rakhot v'hodaot meata v'ad olam.

13 יִשְׁתַּבַּח שִׁמְךָ לָעַד מַלְכֵּנוּ, הָאֵל הַמֶּלֶךְ הַגָּדוֹל
14 וְהַקָּדוֹשׁ בַּשָּׁמַיִם וּבָאָרֶץ, כִּי לְךָ נָאֶה, יְיָ אֱלֹהֵינוּ
15 וֵאלֹהֵי אֲבוֹתֵינוּ, שִׁיר וּשְׁבָחָה, הַלֵּל וְזִמְרָה,
16 עֹז וּמֶמְשָׁלָה, נֶצַח, גְּדֻלָּה וּגְבוּרָה, תְּהִלָּה
17 וְתִפְאֶרֶת, קְדֻשָּׁה וּמַלְכוּת, בְּרָכוֹת וְהוֹדָאוֹת
18 מֵעַתָּה וְעַד עוֹלָם.

Y'hal'lukha Adonai Eloheynu kol maasekha, vakhasidekha, v'tsadikim osey r'tsonekha, v'amkha beyt Yisrael kulam b'rina yodu, vivarkhu vishabkhu, vifaaru et shem k'vodekha ki l'kha tov l'hodot, ulshimkha naim l'zamer, umeolam v'ad olam ata El, barukh ata Adonai, Melekh m'hulal batishbakhot.

19 יְהַלְלוּךָ יְיָ אֱלֹהֵינוּ כָּל מַעֲשֶׂיךָ, וַחֲסִידֶיךָ,
20 וְצַדִּיקִים עוֹשֵׂי רְצוֹנֶךָ, וְעַמְּךָ בֵּית יִשְׂרָאֵל
21 כֻּלָּם בְּרִנָּה יוֹדוּ, וִיבָרְכוּ וִישַׁבְּחוּ, וִיפָאֲרוּ אֶת
22 שֵׁם כְּבוֹדֶךָ; כִּי לְךָ טוֹב לְהוֹדוֹת, וּלְשִׁמְךָ נָעִים
23 לְזַמֵּר, וּמֵעוֹלָם וְעַד עוֹלָם אַתָּה אֵל. בָּרוּךְ אַתָּה
24 יְיָ, מֶלֶךְ מְהֻלָּל בַּתִּשְׁבָּחוֹת:

1 **You Who dwell** in eternity, exalted and holy is Your Name. And it is written: Rejoice in the Eternal, you righteous, for it is fitting for the upright to speak His praise."

3 By the mouth of the upright You shall be praised, and by the words of the righteous You shall be praised; by the tongue of the pious You shall be exalted, and in the midst of the holy You shall be hallowed.

7 **In the assemblies** of the multitudes of Your people, the House of Israel, Your Name, O our Ruler, shall be glorified with song in every generation. For it is the duty of all creatures to give thanks, to praise, to exalt, to bless, to adore, and to extol You, O Eternal our God, and the God of our ancestors, in the words of the songs and psalms of David the son of Jesse, Your anointed servant.

13 **Praised be Your Name** forever, our Ruler, O God, Who rules and is great and holy in the heavens and on the earth; for to You, Eternal our God and God of our ancestors, it is befitting to render song and praise, prayer and psalms, expressing strength and rule, victory, glory and might, praise and beauty, holiness and sovereignty, blessings and thanksgivings, from now and forever.

19 **All Your creations**, O Eternal, shall praise You; Your pious servants, the righteous who do Your will, indeed all Your people the House of Israel, with joyful song shall give thanks, bless, praise, glorify, extol, revere, sanctify, and enthrone Your Name, O our King, for unto You it is good to give thanks, and unto Your Name it is proper to sing praises, for You are God from everlasting to everlasting. Praised are You, Eternal, King extolled in praises.

THE FOURTH CUP

1 **Barukh** ata Adonai, Eloheynu Melekh Haolam, borey pri hagafen.

1 **בָּרוּךְ** אַתָּה יְיָ, אֱלֹהֵינוּ מֶלֶךְ הָעוֹלָם, בּוֹרֵא
2 פְּרִי הַגָּפֶן:

Drink the wine while reclining on the left.

3 **Barukh** ata Adonai, Eloheynu Melekh Haolam, al hagefen v'al pri hagefen, v'al t'nuvat hasade, v'al erets khemda tova ur'khava, sheratsita v'hinkhalta laavoteynu, leekhol mipirya v'lisboa mituva, rakhem na Adonai Eloheynu al Yisrael amekha, v'al Y'rushalayim irekha, v'al Tsiyon mishkan k'vodekha, v'al mizb'khekha v'al heykhalekha, uv'ney Y'rushalayim ir haKodesh bimhera v'yameynu, v'haalenu l'tokha, v'samkhenu b'vinyana, v'nokhal mipirya v'nisba mituva, un'varekh'kha ale-ha bik'dusha uvtohora (on Shabat: ur'tsey v'hakhalitsenu b'yom haShabat hazeh), v'samkhenu b'yom khag hamatsot hazeh, ki ata Adonai tov umetiv lakol, v'node l'kha al haarets v'al pri gafna.

3 **בָּרוּךְ** אַתָּה יְיָ, אֱלֹהֵינוּ מֶלֶךְ הָעוֹלָם, עַל
4 הַגֶּפֶן וְעַל פְּרִי הַגָּפֶן, וְעַל תְּנוּבַת הַשָּׂדֶה,
5 וְעַל אֶרֶץ חֶמְדָּה טוֹבָה וּרְחָבָה, שֶׁרָצִיתָ
6 וְהִנְחַלְתָּ לַאֲבוֹתֵינוּ, לֶאֱכֹל מִפִּרְיָהּ וְלִשְׂבֹּעַ
7 מִטּוּבָהּ. רַחֵם נָא יְיָ אֱלֹהֵינוּ עַל יִשְׂרָאֵל עַמֶּךָ,
8 וְעַל יְרוּשָׁלַיִם עִירֶךָ, וְעַל צִיּוֹן מִשְׁכַּן כְּבוֹדֶךָ,
9 וְעַל מִזְבְּחֶךָ וְעַל הֵיכָלֶךָ. וּבְנֵה יְרוּשָׁלַיִם עִיר
10 הַקֹּדֶשׁ בִּמְהֵרָה בְיָמֵינוּ, וְהַעֲלֵנוּ לְתוֹכָהּ,
11 וְשַׂמְּחֵנוּ בְּבִנְיָנָהּ, וְנֹאכַל מִפִּרְיָהּ וְנִשְׂבַּע
12 מִטּוּבָהּ, וּנְבָרֶכְךָ עָלֶיהָ בִּקְדֻשָּׁה וּבְטָהֳרָה
13 (בשבת: וּרְצֵה וְהַחֲלִיצֵנוּ בְּיוֹם הַשַּׁבָּת הַזֶּה).
14 וְשַׂמְּחֵנוּ בְּיוֹם חַג הַמַּצוֹת הַזֶּה, כִּי אַתָּה יְיָ
15 טוֹב וּמֵטִיב לַכֹּל, וְנוֹדֶה-לְּךָ עַל הָאָרֶץ וְעַל
16 פְּרִי גַפְנָהּ.

78

THE FOURTH CUP

1 **Praised are You**, Eternal our God, Ruler of the universe, Creator of the fruit of the vine.

Drink the wine while reclining on the left.

3 **Praised are you**, Eternal our God, Ruler of the universe, for the vine, and for the fruit of the vine, for the produce of the field and for that precious, good, and spacious land which You gave to our ancestors, to eat of its fruit, and to enjoy its goodness. Have compassion, O Eternal our God, upon us, upon Israel Your people, upon Jerusalem Your city, on Zion the abode of Your glory, and upon Your altar and Your Temple. Rebuild Jerusalem, Your holy city, speedily in our days. Bring us there, and cheer us with her rebuilding; may we eat of her fruit and enjoy her blessings; and we will bless You for this in holiness and purity (*On the Sabbath add:* Be gracious to us and give us strength on this Sabbath day.) Grant us joy on this Festival of Matzoth, for You, O God, are good and beneficent to all; and we therefore give thanks unto You for the land and the fruit of the vine. Praised are You, Eternal, for the land and the fruit of the vine.

נִרְצָה NIRTZA

CONCLUSION OF THE SEDER

Khasal sidur pesakh k'hilkhato, k'khol mishpato v'khukato, kaasher zakhinu l'sader oto, ken nizke laasoto, zakh shokhen m'ona, komem k'hal adat mi mana, b'karov nahel nitey khana, p'duyim l'tsiyon b'rina.

חֲסַל סִדּוּר פֶּסַח כְּהִלְכָתוֹ, כְּכָל מִשְׁפָּטוֹ וְחֻקָּתוֹ. כַּאֲשֶׁר זָכִינוּ לְסַדֵּר אוֹתוֹ, כֵּן נִזְכֶּה לַעֲשׂוֹתוֹ. זָךְ שׁוֹכֵן מְעוֹנָה, קוֹמֵם קְהַל עֲדַת מִי מָנָה. בְּקָרוֹב נַהֵל נִטְעֵי כַנָּה, פְּדוּיִים לְצִיּוֹן בְּרִנָּה.

L'SHANA HABA'AH B'YIRUSHALAYIM.

לְשָׁנָה הַבָּאָה בִּירוּשָׁלָיִם.

On the first night:

Uvkhen **"vay'hi bakhatsi halayla"**

וּבְכֵן "וַיְהִי בַּחֲצִי הַלַּיְלָה"

Az rov nisim hifleyta balayla, b'rosh ashmurot ze halayla, ger tsedek nitsakhto k'nekhelak lo layla.

    Vay'hi bakhatsi halayla.

אָז רֹב נִסִּים הִפְלֵאתָ בַּלַּיְלָה, בְּרֹאשׁ אַשְׁמוּרוֹת זֶה הַלַּיְלָה, גֵּר צֶדֶק נִצַּחְתּוֹ כְּנֶחֱלַק לוֹ לַיְלָה,
וַיְהִי בַּחֲצִי הַלַּיְלָה.

Danta melekh Grar bakhalom halayla, hifkhadta arami b'emesh layla, vayasar Yisrael l'malakh vayukhal lo layla.

    Vay'hi bakhatsi halayla.

דַּנְתָּ מֶלֶךְ גְּרָר בַּחֲלוֹם הַלַּיְלָה, הִפְחַדְתָּ אֲרַמִּי בְּאֶמֶשׁ לַיְלָה, וַיָּשַׂר יִשְׂרָאֵל לְמַלְאָךְ וַיּוּכַל לוֹ לַיְלָה,
וַיְהִי בַּחֲצִי הַלַּיְלָה.

Zera b'khorey fatros makhatsta bakhatsi halayla, kheylam lo matsu b'kumam balayla, tisat n'gid kharoshet silita b'khokhvey layla.

    Vay'hi bakhatsi halayla.

זֶרַע בְּכוֹרֵי פַתְרוֹס מָחַצְתָּ בַּחֲצִי הַלַּיְלָה, חֵילָם לֹא מָצְאוּ בְּקוּמָם בַּלַּיְלָה, טִיסַת נְגִיד חֲרֹשֶׁת סִלִּיתָ בְּכוֹכְבֵי לַיְלָה,
וַיְהִי בַּחֲצִי הַלַּיְלָה.

NIRTZA

CONCLUSION OF THE SEDER

1 **Ended is the Passover seder** according to custom, statute, and law. As we were worthy to celebrate it this year, so may we perform it in future years. O Pure One in heaven above, restore the congregation of Israel in Your love. Speedily lead Your redeemed people to Zion in joy.

6 **NEXT YEAR IN JERUSALEM**

On the first night:

7 **And thus it happened at midnight.**

8 Of old, most of the wonders You did perform at night.
  At the head of the watches is this very night.

Full victory came to Abraham,
  When he divided his company that night.
    It happened at midnight.

10 You judged the king of Gerar in a dream at night;

You frightened Laban in the midst of the night;

And Israel wrestled with God and prevailed at night.
    It happened at midnight.

13 You struck down the firstborn of Egypt at midnight;

And terrified Midian with a loaf of bread in a dream at night;
The armies of Sisera You swept away by the stars of the night.
    It happened at midnight.

#		#	
1	Yaats m'kharef l'nofef ivui, hovashta p'garav balayla, kara bel umatsavo. B'ishon layla, l'ish khamudot nigla raz khazut layla.	1	יָעַץ מְחָרֵף לְנוֹפֵף אִוּוּי, הוֹבַשְׁתָּ פְגָרָיו בַּלַּיְלָה,
		2	כָּרַע בֵּל וּמַצָּבוֹ בְּאִישׁוֹן לַיְלָה, לְאִישׁ חֲמוּדוֹת
		3	נִגְלָה רָז חֲזוּת לַיְלָה,
	Vay'hi bakhatsi halayla.		וַיְהִי בַּחֲצִי הַלָּיְלָה.
4	Mishtaker bikhley kodesh neherag bo balayla, nosha mibor arayot poter biatutey layla, sina natar agagi v'khatav sfarim valayla.	4	מִשְׁתַּכֵּר בִּכְלֵי קֹדֶשׁ נֶהֱרַג בּוֹ בַּלַּיְלָה, נוֹשַׁע
		5	מִבּוֹר אֲרָיוֹת פּוֹתֵר בִּעֲתוּתֵי לַיְלָה, שִׂנְאָה נָטַר
		6	אֲגָגִי וְכָתַב סְפָרִים בַּלַּיְלָה,
	Vay'hi bakhatsi halayla.		וַיְהִי בַּחֲצִי הַלָּיְלָה.
7	Orarta nitskhakha alav b'neded shnat layla, pura tidrokh l'shomer ma milaila, tsarakh kashomer v'sakh ata voker v'gam layla.	7	עוֹרַרְתָּ נִצְחֲךָ עָלָיו בְּנֶדֶד שְׁנַת לַיְלָה, פּוּרָה
		8	תִדְרוֹךְ לְשׁוֹמֵר מַה מִלַּיְלָה, צָרַח כַּשֹּׁמֵר וְשָׂח
		9	אָתָא בֹקֶר וְגַם לָיְלָה,
	Vay'hi bakhatsi halayla.		וַיְהִי בַּחֲצִי הַלָּיְלָה.
	Karev yom asher hu lo yom v'lo layla, ram hoda ki l'kha hayom af l'kha halayla, shomrim hafked l'irkha kol hayom v'khol halayla, tair k'or yom kheshkat layla.	10	קָרֵב יוֹם אֲשֶׁר הוּא לֹא יוֹם וְלֹא לַיְלָה, רָם
		11	הוֹדַע כִּי לְךָ הַיּוֹם אַף לְךָ הַלָּיְלָה, שׁוֹמְרִים
		12	הַפְקֵד לְעִירְךָ כָּל הַיּוֹם וְכָל הַלַּיְלָה, תָּאִיר כְּאוֹר
		13	יוֹם חֶשְׁכַּת לָיְלָה,
	Vay'hi bakhatsi halayla.		וַיְהִי בַּחֲצִי הַלָּיְלָה:

On the second night:

		#	
Uvkhen "vaamartem zevakh pesakh"		14	וּבְכֵן "וַאֲמַרְתֶּם זֶבַח פֶּסַח"
Omets gvurotekha hifleyta bapesakh, b'rosh kol moadot niseyta pesakh, gilita l'ezrakhi khatsot leyl pesakh.		15	אֹמֶץ גְּבוּרוֹתֶיךָ הִפְלֵאתָ בַּפֶּסַח, בְּרֹאשׁ כָּל
		16	מוֹעֲדוֹת נִשֵּׂאתָ פֶּסַח, גִּלִּיתָ לְאֶזְרָחִי חֲצוֹת
		17	לֵיל פֶּסַח,
Vaamartem zevakh pesakh.			וַאֲמַרְתֶּם זֶבַח פֶּסַח.
Dlatav dafakta k'khom hayom bapesakh, hisid nots'tsim ugot matsot bapesakh, v'el habakar rats zekher l'shor erekh pesakh.		18	דְּלָתָיו דָּפַקְתָּ כְּחֹם הַיּוֹם בַּפֶּסַח, הִסְעִיד
		19	נוֹצְצִים עֻגוֹת מַצּוֹת בַּפֶּסַח, וְאֶל הַבָּקָר רָץ זֵכֶר
		20	לְשׁוֹר עֵרֶךְ פֶּסַח,
Vaamartem zevakh pesakh.			וַאֲמַרְתֶּם זֶבַח פֶּסַח.

1   The Assyrian armies besieging Jerusalem were stricken at night; Bel and his pedestal were overthrown in the darkness of night; to Daniel You revealed Your mysteries at night.

It happened at midnight.

4   King Belshazzar of Babylon become drunk of the holy vessels was slain at night; Daniel saved from the lions' den interpreted the terrifying dreams of the night; Haman wrote his edicts of hate at night.

It happened at midnight.

7   You achieved your victory over him in the sleeplessness of Ahasuerus at night; You will tread the winepress for them that ask: "Watchman, what of the night?"

Like the watchman, may he cry out: "The morning has come even as the night."

It happened at midnight.

10   May the day draw near which is neither day nor night. O God, make known that Yours is the day and also the night. Appoint guards over Your city all day and all night. Make bright like the day the darkness of the night.

It happened at midnight.

On the second night:

14   **And say: This is the Passover festval.**

15   Your mighty power You did reveal on Passover. Above all festivals You did exalt the Passover. To Abraham You were revealed at midnight on Passover.

This is the Passover festval.

18   At the heat of the day You knocked at his doors on Passover. He prepared for his visitors cakes of unleavened bread on Passover. And he ran to the herd in anticipation of what we read on Passover.

This is the Passover festval.

Zoamu Sdomim v'lohatu baesh baPesakh, khulats lot mehem, umatsot afa b'kets pesakh, titeyta admat mof v'nof b'ovr'kha baPesakh.	1 זֹעֲמוּ סְדוֹמִים וְלֹהֲטוּ בָאֵשׁ בַּפֶּסַח, חֻלַּץ לוֹט 2 מֵהֶם, וּמַצּוֹת אָפָה בְּקֵץ פֶּסַח, טִאטֵאתָ אַדְמַת 3 מֹף וְנֹף בְּעָבְרְךָ בַּפֶּסַח,
Vaamartem zevakh pesakh.	וַאֲמַרְתֶּם זֶבַח פֶּסַח.
Ya, rosh kol on makhatsta b'leyl shimur pesakh, kabir, al ben b'khor pasakhta b'dam pesakh, l'vilti tet mashkhit lavo bif'takhai bapesakh.	4 יָהּ, רֹאשׁ כָּל אוֹן מָחַצְתָּ בְּלֵיל שִׁמּוּר פֶּסַח, 5 כַּבִּיר, עַל בֵּן בְּכוֹר פָּסַחְתָּ בְּדַם פֶּסַח, לְבִלְתִּי 6 תֵּת מַשְׁחִית לָבֹא בִּפְתָחַי בַּפֶּסַח,
Vaamartem zevakh pesakh.	וַאֲמַרְתֶּם זֶבַח פֶּסַח.
M'sugeret sugara b'itotey pesakh, nishm'da Midyan bitslil s'orey omer pesakh, sorfu mishmaney pul v'lud bikad y'kod pesakh.	7 מְסֻגֶּרֶת סֻגָּרָה בְּעִתּוֹתֵי פֶּסַח, נִשְׁמְדָה מִדְיָן 8 בִּצְלִיל שְׂעוֹרֵי עֹמֶר פֶּסַח, שֹׂרְפוּ מִשְׁמַנֵּי פּוּל 9 וְלוּד בִּיקַד יְקוֹד פֶּסַח,
Vaamartem zevakh pesakh.	וַאֲמַרְתֶּם זֶבַח פֶּסַח.
Od hayom b'nov laamod, ad gaa onat pesakh, pas yad katva l'kakeya tsul bapesakh, tsafo hatsafit arokh hashulkhan bapesakh.	10 עוֹד הַיּוֹם בְּנֹב לַעֲמֹד, עַד גָּעָה עוֹנַת פֶּסַח, פַּס 11 יַד כָּתְבָה לְקַעֲקֵעַ צוּל בַּפֶּסַח, צָפֹה הַצָּפִית 12 עָרוֹךְ הַשֻּׁלְחָן בַּפֶּסַח,
Vaamartem zevakh pesakh.	וַאֲמַרְתֶּם זֶבַח פֶּסַח.
Kahal kinsa Hadasa tsom l'shalesh bapesakh, rosh mibeyt rasha makhatsta b'ets khamishim bapesakh, shtey ele rega, tavi l'utsit bapesakh, taoz yadkha vatarum y'minekha, k'leyl hitkadesh khag pesakh.	13 קָהָל כִּנְּסָה הֲדַסָּה צוֹם לְשַׁלֵּשׁ בַּפֶּסַח, רֹאשׁ 14 מִבֵּית רָשָׁע מָחַצְתָּ בְּעֵץ חֲמִשִּׁים בַּפֶּסַח, שְׁתֵּי 15 אֵלֶּה רֶגַע, תָּבִיא לְעוּצִית בַּפֶּסַח, תָּעֹז יָדְךָ 16 וְתָרוּם יְמִינֶךָ, כְּלֵיל הִתְקַדֶּשׁ חַג פֶּסַח,
Vaamartem zevakh pesakh.	וַאֲמַרְתֶּם זֶבַח פֶּסַח.

1 The Sodomites provoked God and were consumed by fire on Passover. Lot separated from them and baked unleavened bread on Passover. You swept the land of Egypt when You passed through it on Passover.

> This is the Passover festval.

4 You did smite the firstborn on the watchnight of Passover. You did pass over Israel's firstborn on Passover. You permitted no destroyer to enter Israel's doors on Passover.

> This is the Passover festval.

7 The walls of Jericho fell on Passover. Midian was destroyed by a loaf of barley bread measuring an omer on Passover. The soldiers of Pul and Lud were burned in a mighty conflagration on Passover.

> This is the Passover festval.

10 Sennacherib met disaster at Zion's gate on Passover. The hand wrote on the wall in Babylon on Passover. The table was set and all arranged on Passover.

> This is the Passover festval.

13 Queen Esther assembled the community to fast three days at Passover. Haman was hanged on the gallows fifty cubits high on Passover. A twofold punishment You will bring on our enemies on Passover. Then Your right hand shall be uplifted as on this hallowed feast of Passover.

> This is the Passover festval.

| KI LO NAE, KI LO YAE | כִּי לוֹ נָאֶה, כִּי לוֹ יָאֶה | 1 |

Adir bim'luka, bakhur kahalakha, g'dudav yomru lo. L'kha ul'kha, l'kha ki l'kha, l'kha af l'kha, l'kha Adonai hamamlakha, ki lo nae, ki lo yae.

אַדִּיר בִּמְלוּכָה, בָּחוּר כַּהֲלָכָה, גְּדוּדָיו יֹאמְרוּ לוֹ: 2
לְךָ וּלְךָ, לְךָ כִּי לְךָ, לְךָ אַף לְךָ, לְךָ יְיָ הַמַּמְלָכָה. 3
כִּי לוֹ נָאֶה, כִּי לוֹ יָאֶה. 4

Dagul bim'luka, hadur kahalakha, vatikav yomru lo. L'kha ul'kha, l'kha ki l'kha, l'kha af l'kha, l'kha Adonai hamamlakha, ki lo nae, ki lo yae.

דָּגוּל בִּמְלוּכָה, הָדוּר כַּהֲלָכָה, וָתִיקָיו יֹאמְרוּ לוֹ: 5
לְךָ וּלְךָ, לְךָ כִּי לְךָ, לְךָ אַף לְךָ, לְךָ יְיָ הַמַּמְלָכָה. 6
כִּי לוֹ נָאֶה, כִּי לוֹ יָאֶה. 7

Zakai bim'luka, khasin kahalakha, tafsrav yomru lo. L'kha ul'kha, l'kha ki l'kha, l'kha af l'kha, l'kha Adonai hamamlakha, ki lo nae, ki lo yae.

זַכַּאי בִּמְלוּכָה, חָסִין כַּהֲלָכָה, טַפְסְרָיו יֹאמְרוּ לוֹ: לְךָ וּלְךָ, לְךָ כִּי לְךָ, לְךָ אַף לְךָ, לְךָ יְיָ הַמַּמְלָכָה. 8 9
כִּי לוֹ נָאֶה, כִּי לוֹ יָאֶה. 10

Yakhid bim'luka, kabir kahalakha, limudav yomru lo. L'kha ul'kha, l'kha ki l'kha, l'kha af l'kha, l'kha Adonai hamamlakha, ki lo nae, ki lo yae.

יָחִיד בִּמְלוּכָה, כַּבִּיר כַּהֲלָכָה, לִמּוּדָיו יֹאמְרוּ לוֹ: 11
לְךָ וּלְךָ, לְךָ כִּי לְךָ, לְךָ אַף לְךָ, לְךָ יְיָ הַמַּמְלָכָה. 12
כִּי לוֹ נָאֶה, כִּי לוֹ יָאֶה. 13

Moshel bim'luka, nora kahalakha, svivav yomru lo. L'kha ul'kha, l'kha ki l'kha, l'kha af l'kha, l'kha Adonai hamamlakha, ki lo nae, ki lo yae.

מוֹשֵׁל בִּמְלוּכָה, נוֹרָא כַּהֲלָכָה, סְבִיבָיו יֹאמְרוּ לוֹ: לְךָ וּלְךָ, לְךָ כִּי לְךָ, לְךָ אַף לְךָ, לְךָ יְיָ הַמַּמְלָכָה. 14 15
כִּי לוֹ נָאֶה, כִּי לוֹ יָאֶה. 16

Anav bim'luka, pode kahalakha, tsadikav yomru lo. L'kha ul'kha, l'kha ki l'kha, l'kha af l'kha, l'kha Adonai hamamlakha, ki lo nae, ki lo yae.

עָנָיו בִּמְלוּכָה, פּוֹדֶה כַּהֲלָכָה, צַדִּיקָיו יֹאמְרוּ לוֹ: 17
לְךָ וּלְךָ, לְךָ כִּי לְךָ, לְךָ אַף לְךָ, לְךָ יְיָ הַמַּמְלָכָה. 18
כִּי לוֹ נָאֶה, כִּי לוֹ יָאֶה. 19

Kadosh bim'luka, rakhum kahalakha, shinanav yomru lo. L'kha ul'kha, l'kha ki l'kha, l'kha af l'kha, l'kha Adonai hamamlakha, ki lo nae, ki lo yae.

קָדוֹשׁ בִּמְלוּכָה, רַחוּם כַּהֲלָכָה, שִׁנְאַנָּיו יֹאמְרוּ לוֹ: לְךָ וּלְךָ, לְךָ כִּי לְךָ, לְךָ אַף לְךָ, לְךָ יְיָ הַמַּמְלָכָה. 20 21
כִּי לוֹ נָאֶה, כִּי לוֹ יָאֶה. 22

Takif bim'luka, tomekh kahalakha, t'mimav yomru lo. L'kha ul'kha, l'kha ki l'kha, l'kha af l'kha, l'kha Adonai hamamlakha, ki lo nae, ki lo yae.

תַּקִּיף בִּמְלוּכָה, תּוֹמֵךְ כַּהֲלָכָה, תְּמִימָיו יֹאמְרוּ לוֹ: לְךָ וּלְךָ, לְךָ כִּי לְךָ, לְךָ אַף לְךָ, לְךָ יְיָ הַמַּמְלָכָה. 23 24
כִּי לוֹ נָאֶה, כִּי לוֹ יָאֶה. 25

1   KI LO NAE, KI LO YAE

2 Mighty in majesty, Supreme indeed!
His legions sing to Him:
Yours alone, O God, is the world's sovereignty.
To Him it is fitting, to Him it is due.

5 First in majesty, Glorious indeed!
His faithful sing to Him:
Yours alone, O God, is the world's sovereignty.
To Him it is fitting, to Him it is due.

8 Pure in majesty, Powerful indeed!
His attendants sing to Him:
Yours alone, O God, is the world's sovereignty
To Him it is fitting, to Him it is due.

11 Unique in majesty, Mighty indeed!
His disciples sing to Him:
Yours alone, O God, is the world's sovereignty.
To Him it is fitting, to Him it is due.

14 Ruling in majesty, Revered indeed!
His angels sing to Him:
Yours alone, O God, is the world's sovereignty.
To Him it is fitting, to Him it is due.

17 Humble in majesty, Redeemer indeed!
His righteous sing to Him!
Yours alone, O God, is the world's sovereignty.
To Him it is fitting, to Him it is due.

20 Holy in majesty, Merciful indeed!
His myriads sing to Him
Yours alone, O God, is the world's sovereignty.
To Him it is fitting, to Him it is due.

23 Almighty in majesty, Sustainer indeed!
His upright sing to Him:
Yours alone, O God, is the world's sovereignty.
To Him it is fitting, to Him it is due.

ADIR HU	**אַדִּיר הוּא**

Adir hu, yivne veyto b'karov, bimhera bimhera bimhera, b'yameynu b'karov, El b'ney, El b'ney, b'ney veytkha b'karov.

אַדִּיר הוּא, יִבְנֶה בֵיתוֹ בְּקָרוֹב, בִּמְהֵרָה בִּמְהֵרָה, בְּיָמֵינוּ בְּקָרוֹב. אֵל בְּנֵה, אֵל בְּנֵה, בְּנֵה בֵיתְךָ בְּקָרוֹב.

Bakhur hu, gadol hu, dagul hu, yivne veyto b'karov, bimhera bimhera, b'yameynu v'karov, El b'ney, El b'ney, b'ney veytkha b'karov.

בָּחוּר הוּא, גָּדוֹל הוּא, דָּגוּל הוּא, יִבְנֶה בֵיתוֹ בְּקָרוֹב, בִּמְהֵרָה בִּמְהֵרָה, בְּיָמֵינוּ בְּקָרוֹב. אֵל בְּנֵה, אֵל בְּנֵה, בְּנֵה בֵיתְךָ בְּקָרוֹב.

Hadur hu, vatik hu, zakai hu, khasid hu, yivne veyto b'karov, bimhera bimhera, b'yameynu v'karov, El b'ney, El b'ney, b'ney veytkha b'karov.

הָדוּר הוּא, וָתִיק הוּא, זַכַּאי הוּא, חָסִיד הוּא, יִבְנֶה בֵיתוֹ בְּקָרוֹב, בִּמְהֵרָה בִּמְהֵרָה, בְּיָמֵינוּ בְּקָרוֹב. אֵל בְּנֵה, אֵל בְּנֵה, בְּנֵה בֵיתְךָ בְּקָרוֹב.

Tahor hu, yakhid hu, kabir hu, lamud hu, Melekh hu, nora hu, sagiv hu, izuz hu, pode hu, tsadik hu, yivne veyto b'karov, bimhera bimhera, b'yameynu v'karov, El b'ney, El b'ney, b'ney veytkha b'karov.

טָהוֹר הוּא, יָחִיד הוּא, כַּבִּיר הוּא, לָמוּד הוּא, מֶלֶךְ הוּא, נוֹרָא הוּא, סַגִּיב הוּא, עִזּוּז הוּא, פּוֹדֶה הוּא, צַדִּיק הוּא, יִבְנֶה בֵיתוֹ בְּקָרוֹב, בִּמְהֵרָה בִּמְהֵרָה, בְּיָמֵינוּ בְּקָרוֹב. אֵל בְּנֵה, אֵל בְּנֵה, בְּנֵה בֵיתְךָ בְּקָרוֹב.

Kadosh hu, rakhum hu, shadai hu, takif hu, yivne veyto b'karov, bimhera bimhera, b'yameynu v'karov, El b'ney, El b'ney, b'ney veytkha b'karov.

קָדוֹשׁ הוּא, רַחוּם הוּא, שַׁדַּי הוּא, תַּקִּיף הוּא, יִבְנֶה בֵיתוֹ בְּקָרוֹב, בִּמְהֵרָה בִּמְהֵרָה, בְּיָמֵינוּ בְּקָרוֹב. אֵל בְּנֵה, אֵל בְּנֵה, בְּנֵה בֵיתְךָ בְּקָרוֹב.

1   **ADIR HU**

2 God is Mighty! May He soon rebuild His Temple.
Speedily, speedily, in our days, soon.
O God, rebuild, O God, rebuild, Rebuild Your Temple soon.

5 God is First, Great, and Renowned!
May He soon rebuild His Temple.
Speedily, speedily, in our days, soon.
O God, rebuild, O God, rebuild, rebuild Your Temple soon.

8 He is Glorious, Faithful, Just, and Gracious!
May He soon rebuild His Temple.
Speedily, speedily, in our days, soon.
O God, rebuild, O God, rebuild, rebuild Your Temple soon.

12 He is Pure, Unique, Mighty, Wise, Majestic, Revered,
Exalted, Strong, Redeemer, and Righteous!
May He soon rebuild His Temple.
Speedily, speedily, in our days, soon.
O God, rebuild, O God, rebuild, rebuild Your Temple soon.

17 He is Holy, Merciful, Powerful, Almighty!
May He soon rebuild His Temple.
Speedily, speedily, in our days, soon.
O God, rebuild, O God, rebuild, rebuild Your Temple soon.

אֶחָד מִי יוֹדֵעַ

Ekhad mi yodeya

Ekhad mi yodeya? Ekhad ani yodeya. Ekhad Eloheynu shebashamayim uva-arets.

אֶחָד מִי יוֹדֵעַ? אֶחָד אֲנִי יוֹדֵעַ: אֶחָד אֱלֹהֵינוּ שֶׁבַּשָּׁמַיִם וּבָאָרֶץ.

Shnayim mi yodeya? Shnayim ani yodeya. Shney lukhot habrit, ekhad Eloheynu shebashamayim uvaarets.

שְׁנַיִם מִי יוֹדֵעַ? שְׁנַיִם אֲנִי יוֹדֵעַ: שְׁנֵי לֻחוֹת הַבְּרִית, אֶחָד אֱלֹהֵינוּ שֶׁבַּשָּׁמַיִם וּבָאָרֶץ.

Shlosha mi yodeya? Shlosha ani yodeya. Shlosha avot, shney lukhot habrit, ekhad Eloheynu shebashamayim uvaarets.

שְׁלֹשָׁה מִי יוֹדֵעַ? שְׁלֹשָׁה אֲנִי יוֹדֵעַ: שְׁלֹשָׁה אָבוֹת, שְׁנֵי לֻחוֹת הַבְּרִית, אֶחָד אֱלֹהֵינוּ שֶׁבַּשָּׁמַיִם וּבָאָרֶץ.

Arba mi yodeya? Arba ani yodeya. Arba imahot, shlosha avot, shney lukhot habrit, ekhad Eloheynu shebashamayim uvaarets.

אַרְבַּע מִי יוֹדֵעַ? אַרְבַּע אֲנִי יוֹדֵעַ: אַרְבַּע אִמָּהוֹת, שְׁלֹשָׁה אָבוֹת, שְׁנֵי לֻחוֹת הַבְּרִית, אֶחָד אֱלֹהֵינוּ שֶׁבַּשָּׁמַיִם וּבָאָרֶץ.

Khamisha mi yodeya? Khamisha ani yodeya. Khamisha khumshey tora, arba imahot, shlosha avot, shney lukhot habrit, ekhad Eloheynu shebashamayim uvaarets.

חֲמִשָּׁה מִי יוֹדֵעַ? חֲמִשָּׁה אֲנִי יוֹדֵעַ: חֲמִשָּׁה חֻמְשֵׁי תוֹרָה, אַרְבַּע אִמָּהוֹת, שְׁלֹשָׁה אָבוֹת, שְׁנֵי לֻחוֹת הַבְּרִית, אֶחָד אֱלֹהֵינוּ שֶׁבַּשָּׁמַיִם וּבָאָרֶץ.

Shisha mi yodeya? Shisha ani yodeya. Shisha sidrey mishna, khamisha khumshey tora, arba imahot, shlosha avot, shney lukhot habrit, ekhad Eloheynu shebashamayim uvaarets.

שִׁשָּׁה מִי יוֹדֵעַ? שִׁשָּׁה אֲנִי יוֹדֵעַ: שִׁשָּׁה סִדְרֵי מִשְׁנָה, חֲמִשָּׁה חֻמְשֵׁי תוֹרָה, אַרְבַּע אִמָּהוֹת, שְׁלֹשָׁה אָבוֹת, שְׁנֵי לֻחוֹת הַבְּרִית, אֶחָד אֱלֹהֵינוּ שֶׁבַּשָּׁמַיִם וּבָאָרֶץ.

Shiva mi yodeya? Shiva ani yodeya. Shiva y'mey shabta, shisha sidrey mishna, khamisha khumshey Torah, arba imahot, shlosha avot, shney lukhot habrit, ekhad Eloheynu shebashamayim uvaarets.

שִׁבְעָה מִי יוֹדֵעַ? שִׁבְעָה אֲנִי יוֹדֵעַ: שִׁבְעָה יְמֵי שַׁבַּתָּא, שִׁשָּׁה סִדְרֵי מִשְׁנָה, חֲמִשָּׁה חֻמְשֵׁי תוֹרָה, אַרְבַּע אִמָּהוֹת, שְׁלֹשָׁה אָבוֹת, שְׁנֵי לֻחוֹת הַבְּרִית, אֶחָד אֱלֹהֵינוּ שֶׁבַּשָּׁמַיִם וּבָאָרֶץ.

1   Who knows one?

2   Who knows one? I know one. One is our God, in heaven and on earth.

4   Who knows two? I know two.

Two are the tablets of the covenant; One is our God, in heaven and on earth.

6   Who knows three? I know three.

Three are the patriarchs; Two are the tablets of the covenant; One is our God, in heaven and on earth.

9   Who knows four? I know four.

Four are the matriarchs; Three are the patriarchs; Two are the tablets of the covenant; One is our God, in heaven and on earth.

12   Who knows five? I know five.

Five are the books of the Torah; Four are the matriarchs;

Three are the patriarchs; Two are the tablets of the covenant; One is our God, in heaven and on earth.

16   Who knows six? I know six.

Six are the sections of the Mishnah; Five are the books of the Torah; Four are the matriarchs; Three are the patriarchs;

Two are the tablets of the covenant; One is our God, in heaven and on earth.

20   Who knows seven? I know seven.

Seven are the days of the week; Six are the sections of the Mishnah; Five are the books of the Torah; Four are the matriarchs; Three are the patriarchs; Two are the tablets of the covenant; One is our God, in heaven and on earth.

Shmona mi yodeya? Shmona ani yodeya. Shmona y'mey mila, shiva y'mey shabta, shisha sidrey mishna, khamisha khumshey tora, arba imahot, shlosha avot, shney lukhot habrit, ekhad Eloheynu shebashamayim uvaarets.	1 **שְׁמוֹנָה** מִי יוֹדֵעַ? שְׁמוֹנָה אֲנִי יוֹדֵעַ: שְׁמוֹנָה 2 יְמֵי מִילָה, שִׁבְעָה יְמֵי שַׁבַּתָּא, שִׁשָּׁה סִדְרֵי 3 מִשְׁנָה, חֲמִשָּׁה חֻמְשֵׁי תוֹרָה, אַרְבַּע אִמָּהוֹת, 4 שְׁלֹשָׁה אָבוֹת, שְׁנֵי לֻחוֹת הַבְּרִית, אֶחָד אֱלֹהֵינוּ 5 שֶׁבַּשָּׁמַיִם וּבָאָרֶץ.
Tisha mi yodeya? Tisha ani yodeya. Tisha yarkhey leda, shmona y'mey mila, shiva y'mey shabta, shisha sidrey mishna, khamisha khumshey tora, arba imahot, shlosha avot, shney lukhot habrit, ekhad Eloheynu shebashamayim uvaarets.	6 **תִּשְׁעָה** מִי יוֹדֵעַ? תִּשְׁעָה אֲנִי יוֹדֵעַ: תִּשְׁעָה 7 יַרְחֵי לֵדָה, שְׁמוֹנָה יְמֵי מִילָה, שִׁבְעָה יְמֵי 8 שַׁבַּתָּא, שִׁשָּׁה סִדְרֵי מִשְׁנָה, חֲמִשָּׁה חֻמְשֵׁי 9 תוֹרָה, אַרְבַּע אִמָּהוֹת, שְׁלֹשָׁה אָבוֹת, שְׁנֵי לֻחוֹת 10 הַבְּרִית, אֶחָד אֱלֹהֵינוּ שֶׁבַּשָּׁמַיִם וּבָאָרֶץ.
Asara mi yodeya? Asara ani yodeya. Asara dibraya, tisha yarkhey leda, shmona y'mey mila, shiva y'mey shabta, shisha sidrey mishna, khamisha khumshey tora, arba imahot, shlosha avot, shney lukhot habrit, ekhad Eloheynu shebashamayim uvaarets.	11 **עֲשָׂרָה** מִי יוֹדֵעַ? עֲשָׂרָה אֲנִי יוֹדֵעַ: עֲשָׂרָה 12 דִבְּרַיָּא, תִּשְׁעָה יַרְחֵי לֵדָה, שְׁמוֹנָה יְמֵי מִילָה, 13 שִׁבְעָה יְמֵי שַׁבַּתָּא, שִׁשָּׁה סִדְרֵי מִשְׁנָה, חֲמִשָּׁה 14 חֻמְשֵׁי תוֹרָה, אַרְבַּע אִמָּהוֹת, שְׁלֹשָׁה אָבוֹת, 15 שְׁנֵי לֻחוֹת הַבְּרִית, אֶחָד אֱלֹהֵינוּ שֶׁבַּשָּׁמַיִם 16 וּבָאָרֶץ.
Akhad asar mi yodeya? Akhad asar ani yodeya. Akhad asar kokhvaya, asara dibraya, tisha yarkhey leda, shmona y'mey mila, shiva y'mey shabta, shisha sidrey mishna, khamisha khumshey tora, arba imahot, shlosha avot, shney lukhot habrit, ekhad Eloheynu shebashamayim uvaarets.	17 **אַחַד עָשָׂר** מִי יוֹדֵעַ? אַחַד עָשָׂר אֲנִי יוֹדֵעַ: אַחַד 18 עָשָׂר כּוֹכְבַיָּא, עֲשָׂרָה דִבְּרַיָּא, תִּשְׁעָה יַרְחֵי 19 לֵדָה, שְׁמוֹנָה יְמֵי מִילָה, שִׁבְעָה יְמֵי שַׁבַּתָּא, 20 שִׁשָּׁה סִדְרֵי מִשְׁנָה, חֲמִשָּׁה חֻמְשֵׁי תוֹרָה, 21 אַרְבַּע אִמָּהוֹת, שְׁלֹשָׁה אָבוֹת, שְׁנֵי לֻחוֹת 22 הַבְּרִית, אֶחָד אֱלֹהֵינוּ שֶׁבַּשָּׁמַיִם וּבָאָרֶץ.

1   Who knows eight? I know eight.

Eight are the days before circumcision; Seven are the days of the week; Six are the sections of the Mishnah; Five are the books of the Torah; Four are the matriarchs;

Three are the patriarchs; Two are the tablets of the covenant; One is our God, in heaven and on earth.

6   Who knows nine? I know nine.

Nine are the months of childbirth; Eight are the days before circumcision; Seven are the days of the week; Six are the sections of the Mishnah; Five are the books of the Torah; Four are the matriarchs; Three are the patriarchs; Two are the tablets of the covenant; One is our God, in heaven and on earth.

11   Who knows ten? I know ten.

Ten are the commandments; Nine are the months of childbirth; Eight are the days before circumcision; Seven are the days of the week; Six are the sections of the Mishnah; Five are the books of the Torah; Four are the matriarchs; Three are the patriarchs; Two are the tablets of the covenant; One is our God, in heaven and on earth.

17   Who knows eleven? I know eleven.

Eleven are the stars in Joseph's dream; Ten are the commandments; Nine are the months of childbirth; Eight are the days before circumcision; Seven are the days of the week; Six are the sections of the Mishnah; Five are the books of the Torah; Four are the matriarchs; Three are the patriarchs; Two are the tablets of the covenant; One is our God, in heaven and on earth.

Shnem asar mi yodeya? Shnem asar ani yodeya. Shnem asar shivtaya, akhad asar kokhvaya, asara dibraya, tisha yarkhey leda, shmona y'mey mila, shiva y'mey shabta, shisha sidrey mishna, khamisha khumshey tora, arba imahot, shlosha avot, shney lukhot habrit, ekhad Eloheynu shebashamayim uvaarets.

שְׁנֵים עָשָׂר מִי יוֹדֵעַ? שְׁנֵים עָשָׂר אֲנִי יוֹדֵעַ: שְׁנֵים עָשָׂר שִׁבְטַיָּא, אַחַד עָשָׂר כּוֹכְבַיָּא, עֲשָׂרָה דִּבְּרַיָּא, תִּשְׁעָה יַרְחֵי לֵדָה, שְׁמוֹנָה יְמֵי מִילָה, שִׁבְעָה יְמֵי שַׁבְּתָא, שִׁשָּׁה סִדְרֵי מִשְׁנָה, חֲמִשָּׁה חֻמְשֵׁי תוֹרָה, אַרְבַּע אִמָּהוֹת, שְׁלֹשָׁה אָבוֹת, שְׁנֵי לֻחוֹת הַבְּרִית, אֶחָד אֱלֹהֵינוּ שֶׁבַּשָּׁמַיִם וּבָאָרֶץ.

Shlosha asar mi yodeya? Shlosha asar ani yodeya. Shlosha asar midaya, shnem asar shivtaya, akhad asar kokhvaya, asara dibraya, tisha yarkhey leda, shmona y'mey mila, shiva y'mey shabta, shisha sidrey mishna, khamisha khumshey tora, arba imahot, shlosha avot, shney lukhot habrit, ekhad Eloheynu shebashamayim uvaarets.

שְׁלֹשָׁה עָשָׂר מִי יוֹדֵעַ? שְׁלֹשָׁה עָשָׂר אֲנִי יוֹדֵעַ: שְׁלֹשָׁה עָשָׂר מִדַּיָּא, שְׁנֵים עָשָׂר שִׁבְטַיָּא, אַחַד עָשָׂר כּוֹכְבַיָּא, עֲשָׂרָה דִּבְּרַיָּא, תִּשְׁעָה יַרְחֵי לֵדָה, שְׁמוֹנָה יְמֵי מִילָה, שִׁבְעָה יְמֵי שַׁבְּתָא, שִׁשָּׁה סִדְרֵי מִשְׁנָה, חֲמִשָּׁה חֻמְשֵׁי תוֹרָה, אַרְבַּע אִמָּהוֹת, שְׁלֹשָׁה אָבוֹת, שְׁנֵי לֻחוֹת הַבְּרִית, אֶחָד אֱלֹהֵינוּ שֶׁבַּשָּׁמַיִם וּבָאָרֶץ.

Khad gadya

חַד גַּדְיָא

Khad gadya, khad gadya, d'zabin aba bitrey zuzey, khad gadya, khad gadya.

חַד גַּדְיָא, חַד גַּדְיָא, דְּזַבִּין אַבָּא בִּתְרֵי זוּזֵי, חַד גַּדְיָא, חַד גַּדְיָא.

V'ata shunra, v'akhla l'gadya, d'zabin aba bitrey zuzey, khad gadya, khad gadya.

וְאָתָא שׁוּנְרָא, וְאָכְלָה לְגַּדְיָא, דְּזַבִּין אַבָּא בִּתְרֵי זוּזֵי, חַד גַּדְיָא, חַד גַּדְיָא.

V'ata kalba, v'nashakh l'shunra, d'akhla l'gadya, d'zabin aba bitrey zuzey, khad gadya, khad gadya.

וְאָתָא כַּלְבָּא, וְנָשַׁךְ לְשׁוּנְרָא, דְּאָכְלָה לְגַּדְיָא, דְּזַבִּין אַבָּא בִּתְרֵי זוּזֵי, חַד גַּדְיָא, חַד גַּדְיָא.

V'ata khutra, v'hika l'khalba, d'nashakh l'shunra, d'akhla l'gadya, d'zabin aba bitrey zuzey, khad gadya, khad gadya.

וְאָתָא חֻטְרָא, וְהִכָּה לְכַלְבָּא, דְּנָשַׁךְ לְשׁוּנְרָא, דְּאָכְלָה לְגַּדְיָא, דְּזַבִּין אַבָּא בִּתְרֵי זוּזֵי, חַד גַּדְיָא, חַד גַּדְיָא.

1 Who knows twelve? I know twelve.

Twelve are the tribes of Israel; Eleven are the stars in Joseph's dream; Ten are the commandments; Nine are the months of childbirth; Eight are the days before circumcision; Seven are the days of the week; Six are the sections of the Mishnah; Five are the books of the Torah; Four are the matriarchs; Three are the patriarchs; Two are the tablets of the covenant; One is our God, in heaven and on earth.

8 Who knows thirteen? I know thirteen.

Thirteen are God's attributes; Twelve are the tribes of Israel; Eleven are the stars in Joseph's dream; Ten are the commandments; Nine are the months of childbirth; Eight are the days before circumcision; Seven are the days of the week; Six are the sections of the Mishnah; Five are the books of the Torah; Four are the matriarchs; Three are the patriarchs; Two are the tablets of the covenant; One is our God, in heaven and on earth.

15   **Khad gadya**

16 One little goat, one little goat, my father bought for two zuzim. One little goat, one little goat.

18 Then came a cat and ate the goat my father bought for two zuzim. One little goat, one little goat.

20 Then came a dog and bit the cat, that ate the goat my father bought for two zuzim. One little goat, one little goat.

22 Then came a stick and beat the dog, that bit the cat that ate the goat my father bought for two zuzim. One little goat, one little goat.

	Transliteration	Hebrew

V'ata nura, v'saraf l'khutra, d'hika l'khalba, d'nashakh l'shunra, d'akhla l'gadya, d'zabin aba bitrey zuzey, khad gadya, khad gadya.

1 וְאָתָא נוּרָא, וְשָׂרַף לְחֻטְרָא, דְּהִכָּה לְכַלְבָּא,
2 דְּנָשַׁךְ לְשֻׁנְרָא, דְּאָכְלָה לְגַדְיָא, דְּזַבִּין אַבָּא
3 בִּתְרֵי זוּזֵי, חַד גַּדְיָא, חַד גַּדְיָא.

V'ata maya, v'khava l'nura, d'saraf l'khutra, d'hika l'khalba, d'nashakh l'shunra, d'akhla l'gadya, d'zabin aba bitrey zuzey, khad gadya, khad gadya.

4 וְאָתָא מַיָּא, וְכָבָה לְנוּרָא, דְּשָׂרַף לְחֻטְרָא,
5 דְּהִכָּה לְכַלְבָּא, דְּנָשַׁךְ לְשֻׁנְרָא, דְּאָכְלָה לְגַדְיָא,
6 דְּזַבִּין אַבָּא בִּתְרֵי זוּזֵי, חַד גַּדְיָא, חַד גַּדְיָא.

V'ata tora, v'shata l'maya, d'khava l'nura, d'saraf l'khutra, d'hika l'khalba, d'nashakh l'shunra, d'akhla l'gadya, d'zabin aba bitrey zuzey, khad gadya, khad gadya.

7 וְאָתָא תּוֹרָא, וְשָׁתָא לְמַיָּא, דְּכָבָה לְנוּרָא,
8 דְּשָׂרַף לְחֻטְרָא, דְּהִכָּה לְכַלְבָּא, דְּנָשַׁךְ לְשֻׁנְרָא,
9 דְּאָכְלָה לְגַדְיָא, דְּזַבִּין אַבָּא בִּתְרֵי זוּזֵי, חַד
10 גַּדְיָא, חַד גַּדְיָא.

V'ata hashokhet, v'shakhat l'tora, d'shata l'maya, d'khava l'nura, d'saraf l'khutra, d'hika l'khalba, d'nashakh l'shunra, d'akhla l'gadya, d'zabin aba bitrey zuzey, khad gadya, khad gadya.

11 וְאָתָא הַשּׁוֹחֵט, וְשָׁחַט לְתוֹרָא, דְּשָׁתָא לְמַיָּא,
12 דְּכָבָה לְנוּרָא, דְּשָׂרַף לְחֻטְרָא, דְּהִכָּה לְכַלְבָּא,
13 דְּנָשַׁךְ לְשֻׁנְרָא, דְּאָכְלָה לְגַדְיָא, דְּזַבִּין אַבָּא
14 בִּתְרֵי זוּזֵי, חַד גַּדְיָא, חַד גַּדְיָא.

V'ata malakh hamavet, v'shakhat l'shokhet, d'shakhat l'tora, d'shata l'maya, d'khava l'nura, d'saraf l'khutra, d'hika l'khalba, d'nashakh l'shunra, d'akhla l'gadya, d'zabin aba bitrey zuzey, khad gadya, khad gadya.

15 וְאָתָא מַלְאַךְ הַמָּוֶת, וְשָׁחַט לְשּׁוֹחֵט, דְּשָׁחַט
16 לְתוֹרָא, דְּשָׁתָא לְמַיָּא, דְּכָבָה לְנוּרָא, דְּשָׂרַף
17 לְחֻטְרָא, דְּהִכָּה לְכַלְבָּא, דְּנָשַׁךְ לְשֻׁנְרָא, דְּאָכְלָה
18 לְגַדְיָא, דְּזַבִּין אַבָּא בִּתְרֵי זוּזֵי, חַד גַּדְיָא, חַד
19 גַּדְיָא.

V'ata Hakadosh Barukh Hu, v'shakhat l'malakh hamavet, d'shakhat l'shokhet, d'shakhat l'tora, d'shata l'maya, d'khava l'nura, d'saraf l'khutra, d'hika l'khalba, d'nashakh l'shunra, d'akhla l'gadya, d'zabin aba bitrey zuzey, khad gadya, khad gadya.

20 וְאָתָא הַקָּדוֹשׁ בָּרוּךְ הוּא, וְשָׁחַט לְמַלְאַךְ
21 הַמָּוֶת, דְּשָׁחַט לְשּׁוֹחֵט, דְּשָׁחַט לְתוֹרָא, דְּשָׁתָא
22 לְמַיָּא, דְּכָבָה לְנוּרָא, דְּשָׂרַף לְחֻטְרָא, דְּהִכָּה
23 לְכַלְבָּא, דְּנָשַׁךְ לְשֻׁנְרָא, דְּאָכְלָה לְגַדְיָא, דְּזַבִּין
24 אַבָּא בִּתְרֵי זוּזֵי, חַד גַּדְיָא, חַד גַּדְיָא.

1 Then came a fire and burned the stick, that beat the dog that bit the cat that ate the goat my father bought for two zuzim. One little goat, one little goat.

4 Then came the water and quenched the fire, that burned the stick that beat the dog that bit the cat that ate the goat my father bought for two zuzim. One little goat, one little goat.

7 Then came an ox and drank the water, that quenched the fire that burned the stick that beat the dog that bit the cat that ate the goat my father bought for two zuzim. One little goat, one little goat.

11 Then came a *shohet* and slaughtered the ox, that drank the water that quenched the fire that burned the stick that beat the dog that bit the cat that ate the goat my father bought for two zuzim. One little goat, one little goat.

15 Then came the angel of death and killed the *shohet*, that slaughtered the ox that drank the water that quenched the fire that burned the stick that beat the dog that bit the cat that ate the goat my father bought for two zuzim. One little goat, one little goat.

20 Then came the Holy One, blessed be He, and slew the angel of death, that killed the *shohet* that slaughtered the ox that drank the water that quenched the fire that burned the stick that beat the dog that bit the cat that ate the goat my father bought for two zuzim. One little goat, one little goat.

A-DEER HU

SOLO:

A-deer hu, a-deer hu..
Yiv-neh vey-so b'ko-rov.

CHORUS:

Bim-hey-roh, bim-hey-roh,
B'yo-mey-nu b'ko-rov.

SOLO:

CHORUS:

Eyl b'ney, Eyl b'ney
B'ney veys-cho b'ko-rov.

2

Bo-chur hu, go-dol hu.
Yiv-neh vey-so b'ko-rov.

3

Do-gul hu, ho-dur hu.
Yiv-neh vey-so b'ko-rov.

4

Vo-sik hu, za-kay hu.
Yiv-neh vey-so b'ko-rov.

5

Cho-sid hu, to-hor hu.
Yiv-neh vey-so b'ko-rov.

6

Yo-chid hu, ka-bir hu.
Yiv-neh vey-so b'ko-rov.

E-CHOD MEE YO-DEY-A?

E-chod mee yo-dea-a?
E-chod anee yo-dey-a.
E-chod Elohey-nu
She-ba-sho-ma-yeem u-vo-o-rets.

Sh'nayeem mee yo-dey-a?
Sh'nayeem anee yo-dey-a.
Sh'ney lu-chos ha-b'ris,
E-chod Elo-hey-nu
She-ba-sho-ma-yeem u-vo-o-rets.

Sh'lo-sho mee yo-dey-a?
Sh'lo-sho anee yo-dey-a.
Sh'lo-sho o-vos
Sh'ney lu-chos ha-b'ris,
E-chod Elo-hey-nu
She-ba-sho-ma-yeem u-vo-o-rets.

Ar-ba mee yo-deay-a?
Ar-ba anee yo-dey-a.
Ar-ba ee-mo-hos,
Sh'lo-sho o-vos,
Sh'ney lu-chos ha-b'ris,
E-chod Elo-hey-nu
She-ba-sho-ma-yeem u-vo-o-rets.

CHAD GAD-YO

Chad gad-yo, chad gad-yo.
Di-ze-van a-bo bis-rey zu-zey
Chad gad-yo, chad gad-yo.
V'o-so shun-ro v'o-chal l'gad yo.

Di-ze-van...

V'so kal-bo v'no-shach l'shun ro
D'o-chal l'gad-yo.

Di-ze-van...

V'so chut ro-v'hi-koh l'chal-bo
D'no-shach l'shun-ro.
D'o-chal l'gad-yo.

Di-ze-van...

V'o-so nu-ro v'so-raf l'chut-ro
D'hi-koh l'chal-bo, d'no-shach l'shun-ro,
D'o-chal l'gad-yo.

Di-ze-van...

V'o-sa ma-yo v'cho-voh l'nu-ro
D'so-raf l'chut-ro, d'hi-koh l'chal-bo,
D'no-shach l'shun-ro,
D'o-chal l'gad-yo.

Di-ze-van...

Ey-lee-yo-hu Ha-no-vee

Ey-lee-yo-hu ha-no-vee,
Ey-lee-yo-hu h-tish-bee,
Ey-lee-yo-hu, Ey-lee-yo-hu,
Ey-lee-yo-hu, ha-gil-o-dee.

Bim-hey-roh, v'yo-mey-nu
Yo-vo ey-ley-nu;
Im Mo-shee-ach ben Dovid.
Im Mo-shee-ach ben Dovid.

Hatikva

Kol-od b-le-vav p'ni-ma.
Nefesh Y'hu-di ho-mi-ya.
Ul'fa-atey miz-rach ka-dima
Ayin l'Tzi-yon tzo-fi-ya.
Od lo av-da tik-va-tey-nu
Ha-tik-va sh'not al-pa-yim
Li-yot am chaf-shi b'-artzenu
B'eretz Tzi-yon viru-shalayim.

MW00651590